AFFIRM
(THE)
WORD

52-WEEK PRAYER JOURNAL FOR WOMEN

MW00577484

BroadStreet Publishing Group, LLC.
Savage, Minnesota, USA
Broadstreetpublishing.com

Affirm the Word: 52-Week Prayer Journal for Women
© 2024 by BroadStreet Publishing®

9781424568093

Typesetting and design by Garborg Design Works | garborgdesign.com
Editorial services by Michelle Winger | literallyprecise.com

Printed in China.

24 25 26 27 28 29 30   7 6 5 4 3 2 1

Introduction

How to Use Your Prayer Journal

Did you know that the Word of God works when you work it? Just like exercise and proper diet is beneficial for weight loss, and taking a few professional courses can help you advance in the workplace, internalizing God's Word is a crucial component of the spiritual growth process in your life as a believer. However, learning *how* to apply the Word to your life is also important. This journal was designed to help you cultivate a key component of that process—prayer!

No one can live the Christian life in their own strength and must call on God daily (sometimes multiple times a day) to help them navigate the highs and lows of life. The primary resource you've been provided to do so is prayer, and this journal was created to help you become more organized, efficient, and intentional in cultivating a daily prayer life.

You probably have several things going on at any point in time. That's why this devotional is formatted to be studied weekly, with the option to jot down additional prayer requests throughout the week. Just like going on a date or an outing with someone special, fellowshipping with God should be something you enjoy doing and look forward to. There are no specific time or location requirements, so when and where you decide to engage this journal is entirely up to you.

Just know that God desires to meet with you every day. He loves you and is always looking forward to showing you how much while listening to the joys, cares, and concerns of your heart. Even if only for a few minutes.

's important to note that this prayer journal isn't about merely *speaking* the Word but *affirming* it! Write down your prayers, God's responses, and any cripture verses and affirmations that inspire you during your prayer time. Then ake time to speak out loud what the Spirit is saying with faith, intention, and ull assurance in that which you are speaking. Rest assured that you **will** begin o see God move in your life in ways you never imagined. Not just material ossessions, because those are easy for God. He absolutely loves spoiling his hildren and has so much in store for you. But he desires that you thrive in very way, specifically with a greater sense of peace, joy, poise, and Godly onfidence as you become more sensitive to the power of his hand at work in our life. And it is so!

Now that you understand the purpose of this journal, take a moment to review he sample pages that provide a visual guide on how to use it. Then think about ow you intend to incorporate those tips each week with the understanding hat this is **your** journal, and you are welcome to use it in the way that works est for you.

Blessings!

A. Marie

It's important to spend a moment and ask God for his take on the things you are seeking to internalize and how you should apply them personally. You are unique with a different background and experiences that shape your point of view. Ask God for his take on the current week's devotion and then write how he may be leading you to apply it here.

This challenges section is your chance to be really transparent about any hinderances to your obedience in this area, so you can place them before God for his guidance.

Reflection

Take a moment to get clear about what this week's devotion is saying to you. Then write how God is leading you to apply it or seek his will.

How I feel God leading me in this area.

God has been dealing with me about how I speak when I get angry for some time now. Sometimes I feel God wants me to just be silent in the moment but sometimes I am really pushed.

The challenges I have faced in this regard.

The biggest challenge has been not feeling the need to defend myself. It is not okay for people to walk over me and I don't know how to address things gracefully when I am wronged.

How I intend to address those challenges as I progress in prayer.

I have laid this issue before God and am open to help on how to better manage my emotions during conflict. I will also continue to pray about this and remain open to God's leading in those moments.

The intention you write here can be as simple or as complicated as you want it to be. Sometimes, just being determined to wait on God's response before you make another move is all you need to do concerning a matter. However, sometimes a hard apology is required, or going back to the drawing board for something that seemed good but doesn't work. The point is to write down what God is leading you to do, so you can be accountable to your word and do it!

PRAYER REQUESTS

The section is the place where you write the petitions and concerns of your heart to God and leave them to his divine resolution. These prayers can be for you or someone you are led to pray for. The important thing is to bring whatever it is to God, trusting that he hears you and is more than able to work out every situation for the highest good of all involved. And it is so!

Positive affirmation

This week I declare I am...

Poised	Confident	Resilient

I'm grateful for...

My peace of mind! I probably should be a basket case but God is so faithful to me and I am thankful that I am still able to genuinely smile through everything that is going on right now!

What I intend to do...

At this point, all I can do is keep looking for things to smile about. Things have been really tough, but there has been a lot of good happening too. I will focus on that, but still be real and try to keep smiling.

Affirmation to speak over myself

I AM joyful and will continue to express gratitude for the GOOD happening in my life!

I AM encouraged. God is in control so all is well!

The affirmations and intention you set in this section is to help reinforce the positive outcome you anticipate as a result of your reflective work. Declarative affirmations should be short and reaffirm who God says you are at the moment, not how you are defined by your circumstance.

Always set an intention by first acknowledging why you are grateful for where you are and what you already know to be true. You are exactly where you are supposed to be, and God loves you just as you are.

You should have already stated your intention for the week's devotion at this point. This is an opportunity to reaffirm your commitment to surrender your will to God concerning the matter.

Use this space to customize your affirmation with your answers to the previous reflection and affirmation spaces. Start your affirmations with "I AM", "I HAVE" and "I BELIEVE" to help solidify your intention. Then take a few moments to say them out loud.

SCRIPTURE KEY

Last but not least, this journal includes select Scriptures which address key issues that are universal to every believer. This Scripture key is in no way an exhaustive concordance. It serves as a resource to help you apply God's Word to your prayers and have a Scriptural reference for your intentions concerning certain devotion topics.

Affirm the Word

Most believers, meaning those who have chosen to follow God's will by making Jesus Christ the Lord of their lives, understand that there is power in the Word of God. However, very few understand the importance of speaking the Word of God, as well as life-affirming words, over their lives every day. That's right, every day. Why? Because every day you are bombarded with negative words, imagery, experiences, and subsequently feelings that rob you of the joy, peace, and blessings afforded to you under grace as a result of your salvation. Right thinking, living, and being does not come about through osmosis. It is not automatic. It requires effort and participation which starts by first speaking the change you want to see and be.

The good news is you won't have to do this alone if you let God help. You can do that by starting each day asking God to lead you, and then verbally affirming your total dependence on his guidance. He promised that his strength would be perfect in you once you let go and surrender your power to him (2 Corinthians 12:9) . If you are ready to surrender, say "yes" and then go!

This week, write down what you know to be true concerning everything God divinely purposed for your life in this season. Then craft a few short "I Am" and "I Have" affirmations out of that vision. Get comfortable reading it throughout the week, and then progress to verbally affirming it over your life before you start your devotionals, or whenever you have a moment.

> With the fruit of a person's mouth his stomach will be satisfied;
> He will be satisfied with the product of his lips.
> Death and life are in the power of the tongue,
> And those who love it will eat its fruit.
>
> PROVERBS 18:20-21 NASB

Reflection

Take a moment to get clear about what this week's devotion is saying to you. Then write how God is leading you to apply it or seek his will.

How I feel God leading me in this area.

....

....

....

The challenges I have faced in this regard.

....

....

....

How I intend to address those challenges as I progress in prayer.

....

....

....

Positive affirmation

This week I declare I am...

I'm grateful for...

What I intend to do...

Affirmation to speak over myself

Prayer requests

Date

Date

Date

Room for New Beginnings

When it comes to moving on or doing something new, most people start with throwing out old clothes, furniture, junk food, and many other material items that they no longer need or that don't fit their new course. During that process, however, just as many people neglect to throw out and replace negative and harmful ways of thinking that have kept them bound.

Lifegiving words and thoughts must align with the new path and purpose God is calling you to. This week, take a moment to write down a few points about the person and purpose God is calling you to in this new season. Endeavor to speak them out loud at least once a day, or as often as needed until they are the primary thoughts that remain embedded in your heart and mind.

Get ready to see more and more of the new things God has already begun. Live in anticipation of the pathways he is yet paving.

> "Forget the former things;
> do not dwell on the past.
> See, I am doing a new thing?
> Now it springs up; do you not perceive it?
> I am making a way in the wilderness
> and streams in the wasteland."
>
> ISAIAH 43:18-19

Reflection

Take a moment to get clear about what this week's devotion is saying to you. Then write how God is leading you to apply it or seek his will.

How I feel God leading me in this area. ....

....

....

....

....

The challenges I have faced in this regard. ....

....

....

....

....

How I intend to address those challenges as I progress in prayer. ....

....

....

....

....

Positive affirmation

This week I declare I am...

I'm grateful for...

What I intend to do...

Affirmation to speak over myself

Prayer requests

Date

Date

Date

Unwavering Faith

When making room for the new, it's important to understand that change won't always be without opposition. Disappointments, setbacks, and even self-doubt can look like permanent roadblocks to well-intentioned plans. However, looks can be deceiving. Only God's promises and presence have any real staying power.

When you endeavor to stand resolute in your faith, trusting that God is sufficient to sustain you through all adversity, you are guaranteed the victory over your circumstances and made victorious through the divine work accomplished in you.

This week, make note of all the good things that are taking place in your life, despite some of the not-so-good things screaming for your attention. Remember that there are always growing pains, and there may be a learning curve when you are starting something new. However, things will get easier as you persevere. Especially while maintaining a joyful attitude.

> In this you rejoice, though now for a little while, if necessary, you have been grieved by various trials, so that the tested genuineness of your faith—more precious than gold that perishes though it is tested by fire—may be found to result in praise and glory and honor at the revelation of Jesus Christ.
>
> 1 PETER 1:6-9 ESV

Reflection

Take a moment to get clear about what this week's devotion is saying to you. Then write how God is leading you to apply it or seek his will.

How I feel God leading me in this area.

....

....

....

....

The challenges I have faced in this regard.

....

....

....

....

How I intend to address those challenges as I progress in prayer.

....

....

....

....

Positive affirmation

This week I declare I am...

I'm grateful for...

What I intend to do...

Affirmation to speak over myself

Prayer requests

Date

Date

Date

Faith Beyond the Senses

Whether you consider yourself to be a new or seasoned believer, one thing you'll understand is the crucial role faith plays in the life of the redeemed. Not just because the Word commands the "just shall live by faith" in Romans 1:17 ("just" meaning those who have been made righteous through the shed blood of Christ), but because there will be so many things that challenge who you are in Christ.

Every day, you will continue to encounter people, places, ideas and even your own thoughts that try to minimize who God is, what he has done in your life, and what he has called you to do. Yet, God's Word instructs you to trust God and lean not on your own understanding (Proverbs 3:5-6), in full assurance that "he" who has begun a good work in you will complete it.

This week, list one or two ways God is moving on your behalf, in light of Hebrews 11:1 and Proverbs 3:5, and continue to give God thanks for the full manifestation of his power at work in your life.

> Faith is the substance of things hoped for, the evidence of things not seen. For by it the elders obtained a good testimony. By faith we understand that the worlds were framed by the word of God, so that the things which are seen were not made of things which are visible.
>
> HEBREWS 11:1-3 NKJV

Reflection

Take a moment to get clear about what this week's devotion is saying to you. Then write how God is leading you to apply it or seek his will.

How I feel God leading me in this area.

....

....

....

....

The challenges I have faced in this regard.

....

....

....

....

How I intend to address those challenges as I progress in prayer.

....

....

....

....

Positive affirmation

This week I declare I am...

I'm grateful for...

What I intend to do...

Affirmation to speak over myself

Prayer requests

Date

Date

Date

Trusting God through Trials

Last week you were challenged with observing God's hand at work in light of Proverbs 3:5. In moving on to verse 6 of that text, here's a question for you: Do you really trust God? Not just in getting you from point A to point B safely, or making sure basic needs are met, but in everything?

Many people compartmentalize their trust for God because that is how they trust others. You know you will get results with some things but tend to make your own plan for things that take longer or don't happen the way you want. However, even though you have the power to make your own way, things still don't usually go the way you plan when you take matters into your own hands.

This week, take a moment to recognize at least one thing that you have been holding on to and release it to God for his divine resolution. Besides, he always works everything out for your highest good, but only when you let him.

> Trust in the Lord with all your heart
> And do not lean on your own understanding.
> In all your ways acknowledge Him,
> And He will make your paths straight.
>
> PROVERBS 3:5-6 NASB

Reflection

Take a moment to get clear about what this week's devotion is saying to you. Then write how God is leading you to apply it or seek his will.

How I feel God leading me in this area.

....

....

....

....

The challenges I have faced in this regard.

....

....

....

....

How I intend to address those challenges as I progress in prayer.

....

....

....

....

Positive affirmation

This week I declare I am...

I'm grateful for...

What I intend to do...

Affirmation to speak over myself

Prayer requests

Date

Date

Date

Transformation Station

People often confuse conversion (instant salvation through one's faith and confession in Jesus Christ), with transformation (gradual, yet consistent change in one's thinking and behavior). Real, lasting transformation takes *work*. It's not in your own strength because righteous, sustainable change is not possible that way. Through the power of the Holy Spirit, you internalize God's Word, speak it over your life without ceasing, and are led by him concerning your life's purpose in the process. Nothing is impossible when your heart is surrendered to God's will *and* you possess a willingness to be transformed into his image through his Word.

Are you a *practicing* believer? Do you have a sincere desire to become all that God has called you to be? Maybe you don't know where to start to ensure lasting and consistent transformation. Upon conversion, there are two critical things to do: 1) be transformed into your new, divine self by renewing your mind, and 2) follow Christ. Transformation takes place via the work of the Holy Spirit in you as you internalize God's Word and renew your mind in the process. And it is so!

This week, ask God to show you how to do your part as you pursue his will. Then, be prepared to write down and do as he leads. You will always be a work in progress. The hope is that your constant evolution is ever toward the image of God and not that of your carnal self. To follow Christ consistently and effectively, you must actively engage in the transformation of your mind.

> Do not be conformed to this world, but be transformed by the renewing of your mind, so that you may prove what the will of God is, that which is good and acceptable and perfect.
>
> ROMANS 12:2 NASB

Reflection

Take a moment to get clear about what this week's devotion is saying to you. Then write how God is leading you to apply it or seek his will.

How I feel God leading me in this area.

....

....

....

....

The challenges I have faced in this regard.

....

....

....

....

How I intend to address those challenges as I progress in prayer.

....

....

....

....

Positive affirmation

This week I declare I am...

I'm grateful for...

What I intend to do...

Affirmation to speak over myself

Prayer requests

Date

Date

Date

Search the Scriptures

Ask God to reveal himself to you in a way you can understand, and he will do it. God means what he says concerning both his character and how you are to love and serve him, either directly or via various teachings through his Word. It is important for you to speak his Word over your life every day, out loud.

Search the Scripture for yourself! You can be transformed into the image of God, by internalizing his Word and engaging in the spiritual practice of speaking *life,* while in pursuit of your divine purpose. Learning and memorizing Scripture, and putting it into practice, will help you to know God better. His Holy Spirit will guide you in power. You are worthy and valued, but you must surrender your will to God's plan for that plan to manifest itself.

This week, make an effort to consistently and prayerfully engaging in the practice of speaking God's Word over your life. This includes the vision birthed in your heart through the Spirit of God. Engaging in this practice for even a few minutes on a given day will empower you to walk in total trust of his ability to transform you into the highest expression of your true self.

> "You search the Scriptures,
> for in them you think you have eternal life;
> and these are they which testify of Me."
>
> JOHN 5:39 NKJV

Reflection

Take a moment to get clear about what this week's devotion is saying to you. Then write how God is leading you to apply it or seek his will.

How I feel God leading me in this area.

....

....

....

....

The challenges I have faced in this regard.

....

....

....

....

How I intend to address those challenges as I progress in prayer.

....

....

....

....

Positive affirmation

This week I declare I am...

I'm grateful for...

What I intend to do...

Affirmation to speak over myself

Prayer requests

Date

Date

Date

Casting Your Burdens

In 1 Peter 5:7, the Word of God encourages you to cast your cares upon God because he cares for you. Do you know how to do that? Maybe you bring your cares to him, but don't really know how to leave them with him. When you cast your burdens on Christ, you can walk away free.

This week, practice repeating this affirmation and ask God for everything you need, believing that he will supply it all. Not only will engaging in this practice bring about tremendous manifestations of God's supernatural intervention in your life, but it will also enable to you remain at peace, maintaining full assurance in God's ability to intervene on your behalf in the process.

When you are tempted to revisit toxic habits like calling people to actively engage in discussions about your problems, or feverishly trying to come up with ways to resolve issues yourself, remember that you are only free when you cast your burdens on Christ and leave them there.

> **Cast all your anxiety on him because he cares for you.**
>
> 1 PETER 5:7 NIV

Reflection

Take a moment to get clear about what this week's devotion is saying to you. Then write how God is leading you to apply it or seek his will.

How I feel God leading me in this area. ....

....

....

....

The challenges I have faced in this regard. ....

....

....

....

How I intend to address those challenges as I progress in prayer. ....

....

....

....

....

Positive affirmation

This week I declare I am...

I'm grateful for...

What I intend to do...

Affirmation to speak over myself

Prayer requests

Date

Date

Date

To the Door and Through It

When you cast your burdens on God, his power will show up. Be encouraged to bring your issues to God and truly wait for him to provide a complete and unequivocal resolution. He doesn't need your assistance in figuring things out. He already knows how he will do it, and he is already assisting you.

God will help you to the degree that you surrender the matter to him. If you trust him to get you *to* the door but not *through* it, you can't blame him if you decide to kick the door in when you arrive on the scene and cause all hell to break loose! Granted, God always knows what you are going to do before you do it. He is merciful and kind, but you are still subject to the consequences of your actions when you take matters into your own hands.

This week, get honest with yourself about the doors have you been tempted to kick in. Can you commit to leave them with God? If so, write a few words that describe each situation and your resolve to leave them with God until they are completely resolved.

> **"Your Father knows what you need before you ask him."**
>
> MATTHEW 6:8 ESV

Reflection

Take a moment to get clear about what this week's devotion is saying to you. Then write how God is leading you to apply it or seek his will.

How I feel God leading me in this area. ....

....

....

....

....

The challenges I have faced in this regard. ....

....

....

....

....

How I intend to address those challenges as I progress in prayer. ....

....

....

....

....

Positive affirmation

This week I declare I am...

I'm grateful for...

What I intend to do...

Affirmation to speak over myself

Prayer requests

Date

Date

Date

Perfect Resolution

When facing a matter, from the smallest issue to the greatest circumstance, truly cast your burden on God by *first* bringing it to him in prayer, not after you've done all you can do. Continue thanking him for his supernatural intervention, and in moments of doubt, speak his Word over the matter with Scriptures about *asking* and *faith*. Do this whenever the matter comes to mind, or when any information contrary to God's favorable and perfect resolution presents itself.

If you've already told someone about the matter, the only follow-up you need to give is that you've cast the burden on God and that you are awaiting his resolution. That's it. There is no need to discuss details, how you're feeling (unless overjoyed with expectation), or vent. God has it, so it's already done. Your works, actions, and dispositions should reflect that at all times.

This week, be mindful of those moments when you feel tempted to take matters into your own hands. In those moments, be ready to continue speaking and believing that God's perfect resolution is on its way, in his time. And it is so!

> Trust in the Lord with all your heart,
> And lean not on your own understanding;
> In all your ways acknowledge Him,
> And He shall direct your paths.
>
> PROVERBS 3:5-6 NKJV

Reflection

Take a moment to get clear about what this week's devotion is saying to you.
Then write how God is leading you to apply it or seek his will.

How I feel God leading me in this area. ....

....

....

....

....

The challenges I have faced in this regard. ....

....

....

....

....

How I intend to address those challenges as I progress in prayer. ....

....

....

....

....

Positive affirmation

This week I declare I am...

I'm grateful for...

What I intend to do...

Affirmation to speak over myself

Prayer requests

Date

Date

Date

Binding and Loosing

Understanding the meaning of "binding and loosing" and learning how to apply it practically in everyday life can be difficult. The first thing to note is that the practice of binding and loosing refers not to *people*, but to *things*—whatsoever not *whosoever*. It considers rites and ceremonies in the Church. Among the Jews, binding and loosing meant *forbidding* and *allowing*. As directed by the Holy Spirit, whatever was bound (declared forbidden and unlawful), was just that, and whatever was loosed (declared lawful and free to use), remained so. The Jews then bound some things which before were loosed and loosed some things which had previously been bound.

Where Jews had no dealings with Gentiles before, it was then determined and declared that no one should be called common or unclean, and that in Christ Jesus and in his Church, there was no distinction as Jew or Gentile. Things that had been bound or loosed, pronounced unlawful or lawful, were confirmed as such by the authority of God—and are to be considered the same by his followers today.

Jesus spoke to his disciples in a way they understood, so they were not at a loss to comprehend what he meant. He can do the same for you. This week, ask him what needs to be bound and loosed in your life and move forward in his will with confidence and conviction.

> "What God has cleansed,
> no longer consider unholy."
>
> ACTS 10:15 NASB

Reflection

Take a moment to get clear about what this week's devotion is saying to you. Then write how God is leading you to apply it or seek his will.

How I feel God leading me in this area. ....

....

....

....

....

The challenges I have faced in this regard. ....

....

....

....

....

How I intend to address those challenges as I progress in prayer. ....

....

....

....

....

Positive affirmation

This week I declare I am...

[ ] [ ] [ ]

I'm grateful for...

What I intend to do...

Affirmation to speak over myself

Prayer requests

Date

Date

Date

Spiritual Warfare

What does the Bible teach regarding spiritual warfare? James 4:7 explains the basic manner in which it should be done. There are two steps to be followed, and neither should be missed. First, and very important, is to submit yourself to God in every way. The second is to resist the enemy, and he will eventually flee. You need the whole armor of God, worn and activated through prayer, in order to successfully stand against the enemy.

There may be times when you have to call on another believer to help you, as you may not be strong enough in your faith to resist the enemy on your own. You can stand when you have the power of the Holy Spirit working in you. You have authority because you are a believer. Your ability to overcome the forces of evil on your own behalf and on behalf of another person comes through the power of Christ.

You have the power of Christ in you to actively engage in spiritual warfare by the power and assistance of the Holy Spirit. This week, submit yourself to God in every part of your life, so that by his Spirit, you can fight and win over the powers of darkness.

> **Submit therefore to God.**
> **But resist the devil, and he will flee from you.**
>
> JAMES 4:7 NASB

Reflection

Take a moment to get clear about what this week's devotion is saying to you. Then write how God is leading you to apply it or seek his will.

How I feel God leading me in this area.

....

....

....

....

The challenges I have faced in this regard.

....

....

....

....

How I intend to address those challenges as I progress in prayer.

....

....

....

....

Positive affirmation

This week I declare I am...

I'm grateful for...

What I intend to do...

Affirmation to speak over myself

Prayer requests

Date

Date

Date

Mount Your Defense

As a believer, you have been given authority to actively engage the enemy and his forces, when empowered by the Spirit of Christ. Your primary instruction to stand against spiritual warfare is to *resist* the devil and his forces, and he will flee. Attempting to engage the enemy in any other way should only take place through the direct leading of God.

It should be noted that this level of spiritual warfare is not for the novice believer, and it should be case-by-case through the leading of the Holy Spirit. You must be clearly, and unequivocally, led by God to engage in direct confrontation (casting out demons) with the enemy and his forces. Take time to meditate on Scriptures about spiritual warfare before you act. When you're ready, move forward in the power of the Holy Spirit.

God has given you the power and authority to overcome the enemy and the forces of this world, but you can only mount your defense by equipping yourself with his armor—for his glory, your good, and the good of others. And it is so!

> "I have given you authority to tread on serpents and scorpions, and over all the power of the enemy, and nothing shall hurt you."
>
> LUKE 10:19 ESV

Reflection

Take a moment to get clear about what this week's devotion is saying to you. Then write how God is leading you to apply it or seek his will.

How I feel God leading me in this area.

....

....

....

....

The challenges I have faced in this regard.

....

....

....

....

How I intend to address those challenges as I progress in prayer.

....

....

....

....

Positive affirmation

This week I declare I am...

I'm grateful for...

What I intend to do...

Affirmation to speak over myself

Prayer requests

Date

Date

Date

Divine Wholeness

As a child of the Most High God (Elohim), you are called to walk in love and obedience to God's will. With this in mind, you need to recognize that you are loving, kind, obedient, respectful, beautiful, smart, and can always make wise choices. You are capable of completing all your work. You can be a leader and a good example. You have the God-given ability to speak with wisdom, knowing when to ask for help and stand in truth.

You can do all things with the help of Jesus Christ. You are a winner who loves God and is called for his purpose, so all things are working for your good. You were created by God in his image; therefore, you are royalty! Your worth, beauty, and value came from God when he created you, and that will not change. God loves you, so you can love others as you love and respect yourself and Christ inside you. You have been blessed with gifts, talents, and abilities to serve God's divine purpose for your life on this earth, but you will not be receptive to his plan for your life until you *believe* you are worthy to walk in it.

This week, take a moment to write down a few positive qualities about yourself. Then, take a few extra minutes to recognize how God is currently using those gifts, talents, abilities, and attributes to serve his purpose, and give him glory!

> **We know that God causes all things to work together for good to those who love God, to those who are called according to His purpose.**
>
> ROMANS 8:28 NASB

Reflection

Take a moment to get clear about what this week's devotion is saying to you. Then write how God is leading you to apply it or seek his will.

How I feel God leading me in this area.

....

....

....

....

The challenges I have faced in this regard.

....

....

....

....

How I intend to address those challenges as I progress in prayer.

....

....

....

....

Positive affirmation

This week I declare I am...

I'm grateful for...

What I intend to do...

Affirmation to speak over myself

Prayer requests

Date

Date

Date

Total Freedom

The power of God is working through you, to free you of every negative influence. All power is given to you for good in your mind, body, and affairs, and you can rightly use that now! Let go of everything that isn't divinely designed for you, and the perfect plan of your life will come to pass.

Smash and demolish, by your spoken word, every untrue record of your subconscious mind. Let those records return to the dust-heap of their native nothingness, for they came from your own vain imaginings. Make new records through Christ within you: records of health, wealth, love, and perfect self-expression.

This week, try your hand at writing a personal affirmation that declares what God says about you, and what he desires to do in your life. Then speak this affirmation with power and full assurance that he who has begun a good work in you will perfect and complete it until Christ returns (Philippians 1:6). Let it be so today!

> I know that you can do all things,
> and that no purpose of yours can be thwarted.
>
> JOB 42:2 ESV

Reflection

Take a moment to get clear about what this week's devotion is saying to you. Then write how God is leading you to apply it or seek his will.

How I feel God leading me in this area.

_____

_____

_____

_____

The challenges I have faced in this regard.

_____

_____

_____

_____

How I intend to address those challenges as I progress in prayer.

_____

_____

_____

_____

Positive affirmation

This week I declare I am...

[ ] [ ] [ ]

I'm grateful for...

What I intend to do...

Affirmation to speak over myself

Prayer requests

Date

Date

Date

Unwavering Faith

How do you know if your faith is authentic like that of Peter and unwavering like that of Shadrach, Meshach, and Abednego? What brought them to the place that even when they were in the very crucible of crisis, in the very center of suffering, they would not turn away from God or renounce their faith?

If you look closely at the different trials Peter went through, you can probably find yourself in most, if not all, of his experiences. There were probably times when your faith was small and feeble, and if you can really be honest, there may have been times you even denied Christ. But even so, all that you have gone through and are maybe going through now is part of the process of developing unwavering faith, so take heart!

This week, take a moment to reflect on a few trials you have walked through, causing you to question your faith. How could you resolve to view the highs and lows as necessities for developing unwavering faith and be more receptive to staying the course through future difficulties?

> **In all this you greatly rejoice, though now for a little while you may have had to suffer grief in all kinds of trials.**
>
> **1 PETER 1:6 NIV**

Reflection

Take a moment to get clear about what this week's devotion is saying to you. Then write how God is leading you to apply it or seek his will.

How I feel God leading me in this area.

....

....

....

....

The challenges I have faced in this regard.

....

....

....

....

How I intend to address those challenges as I progress in prayer.

....

....

....

....

Positive affirmation

This week I declare I am...

I'm grateful for...

What I intend to do...

Affirmation to speak over myself

Prayer requests

Date

Date

Date

Trial and Fire

When Peter talks about the trials, sorrows, and sufferings experienced in the Christian life, it is because all that he went through—the challenges he faced in the storms, the denial of Christ, and the rebuke he received—was a part of his development. To be "sifted as wheat" meant that Peter would go through great suffering. Why? Because of the value of his faith.

Your faith is of incredible value. Peter's faith was so valuable that Jesus allowed it to be tested by fire. That is why Jesus did not keep Satan from sifting Peter, but instead interceded through prayer that Peter would not only overcome but that he would strengthen others. That is what we see Peter doing in the letters he wrote: encouraging believers through what he learned by trial and fire. Be encouraged to do the same!

This week, think about a time you felt as though you had been sifted like wheat. What did you learn in the fire of trials? Can you see purpose in the suffering you have walked through? How has it encouraged you in your present walk?

> "Simon, Simon, Satan has asked to sift all of you as wheat. But I have prayed for you, Simon, that your faith may not fail. And when you have turned back, strengthen your brothers."
>
> LUKE 22:31-32 NIV

Reflection

Take a moment to get clear about what this week's devotion is saying to you. Then write how God is leading you to apply it or seek his will.

How I feel God leading me in this area.

....

....

....

....

The challenges I have faced in this regard.

....

....

....

....

How I intend to address those challenges as I progress in prayer.

....

....

....

....

Positive affirmation

This week I declare I am...

I'm grateful for...

What I intend to do...

Affirmation to speak over myself

Prayer requests

Date

Date

Date

Even Then

Peter shared the elements that helped develop his faith. These are the things he learned through his personal failures and struggles. But there is a deeper reason God allowed Peter to go through those trials: the same reason he allows you to go through yours. It's not just to give you faith that will move mountains, although that is one of the promises. It's also not just to receive whatever you ask for.

If you move a mountain because of your faith, great! Give God praise. If you receive what you prayed for: a new home, a new job, a new car, an awesome marriage, a beautiful family, a healthy financial portfolio, awesome! Praise God! But if you are in a season of difficulty, of dryness and disappointment, of loss, hurt, shattered dreams, unanswered questions, or unanswered prayer, and you can still give God glory and honor and believe him through it all, *that* is unwavering faith.

Every trial you go through is meant to bring you to a place where you give God praise, glory, and honor—no matter what the outcome. Let it be so! This week, write down three things you can give God praise for despite any negativity that seems prominent in your life. Meditate on these things until you feel ready to offer God praise, causing the atmosphere, and your disposition, to shift. Hallelujah!

> These have come so that the proven genuineness of your faith—
> of greater worth than gold, which perishes even though refined by fire—
> may result in praise, glory and honor when Jesus Christ is revealed.
>
> 1 PETER 1:7 NIV

Reflection

Take a moment to get clear about what this week's devotion is saying to you. Then write how God is leading you to apply it or seek his will.

How I feel God leading me in this area.

....

....

....

....

The challenges I have faced in this regard.

....

....

....

....

How I intend to address those challenges as I progress in prayer.

....

....

....

....

Positive affirmation

This week I declare I am...

[ ] [ ] [ ]

I'm grateful for...

....

....

....

....

What I intend to do...

....

....

....

....

Affirmation to speak over myself

Prayer requests

Date

Date

Date

As Pure Gold

The three Hebrew boys made the most profound statement in Daniel 3:17-18 after being threatened with being thrown into a fiery furnace. "The God we serve is able to deliver us from it... but even if he does not... we will not serve your gods or worship the image of gold you have set up." It did not matter to the friends if God delivered them or left them, they would still give him glory and honor and remain steadfast in their values because the reward of their faith was God.

If you are in the crucible of a crisis, in the very center of suffering, trust that God is with you in the furnace and know that despite the outcome, you will come out as pure gold with unwavering faith.

When you are weighed down by trouble, look to God for comfort and strength, knowing that he promised never to leave or forsake you no matter what! This week, ask a trusted believer to pray with you and believe that you can patiently endure any suffering before you because the reward of your faith is promised by God.

> If anyone builds on the foundation with gold, silver, precious stones, wood, hay, straw—each one's work will become manifest, for the Day will disclose it, because it will be revealed by fire, and the fire will test what sort of work each one has done.
>
> 1 CORINTHIANS 3:12-13 ESV

Reflection

Take a moment to get clear about what this week's devotion is saying to you. Then write how God is leading you to apply it or seek his will.

How I feel God leading me in this area.

....

....

....

....

The challenges I have faced in this regard.

....

....

....

....

How I intend to address those challenges as I progress in prayer.

....

....

....

....

Positive affirmation

This week I declare I am...

I'm grateful for...

What I intend to do...

Affirmation to speak over myself

Prayer requests

Date

Date

Date

True Forgiveness

What is forgiveness? Do you think of it as letting go of offense *and* forgetting it? Although it seems reasonable to protect yourself from future hurt by remembering the offense, it is not in alignment with God's Word. God forgives and forgets, blotting out the offense entirely. And isn't that the way you want it to be when you mess up? You beg for his forgiveness and hope that he completely lets the offense go. Yet, you find it hard to offer the same grace to others.

It's only human to fear that you will be wronged, hurt, used, or abused again, but you must find a way to set that aside and forgive completely just as you want God to forgive you. Remember: you do not have a spirit of fear. You are called to walk by faith and not by sight or perception. Trust that God has you and submit any resistance you have about forgiving someone to God for his guidance and assistance.

This week, think about how you can choose true forgiveness. Can you let an offense go and choose not to remember it? How can you release someone from an offense and walk in the kind of forgiveness that you want from God?

> "If you forgive other people for their offenses, your heavenly Father will also forgive you."
>
> MATTHEW 6:14 NASB

Reflection

Take a moment to get clear about what this week's devotion is saying to you. Then write how God is leading you to apply it or seek his will.

How I feel God leading me in this area.

....

....

....

....

The challenges I have faced in this regard.

....

....

....

....

How I intend to address those challenges as I progress in prayer.

....

....

....

....

Positive affirmation

This week I declare I am...

I'm grateful for...

What I intend to do...

Affirmation to speak over myself

Prayer requests

Date

Date

Date

Not Going Back

Once you truly learn something beneficial, it is very hard to unlearn it and perform that function in a way that disadvantaged you in the past. For example, once you learn how to eat healthy and experience the benefits of your new eating habits, it's difficult to go back to a lifestyle that left you sick, drained, and feeling bad about yourself.

The same can be said for learning how to love and accept people. Once you learn that real love is not about trying to either change someone or bend and twist yourself inside out like a pretzel to be accepted, you will become immune to all the hurt and resentment brought about through others' actions. True acceptance doesn't resist or manipulate; rather, it accepts and shows mercy.

This week, practice acceptance by assessing the information you've learned about someone and decide whether to engage and connect (relate) or disengage (release) and continue to walk your path without criticism or condemnation of that person or the way they choose to live.

> "Whenever you stand praying, forgive, if you have anything against anyone, so that your Father who is in heaven will also forgive you for your offenses."
>
> MARK 11:25 NASB

Reflection

Take a moment to get clear about what this week's devotion is saying to you. Then write how God is leading you to apply it or seek his will.

How I feel God leading me in this area.

....

....

....

....

The challenges I have faced in this regard.

....

....

....

....

How I intend to address those challenges as I progress in prayer.

....

....

....

....

Positive affirmation

This week I declare I am...

I'm grateful for...

What I intend to do...

Affirmation to speak over myself

Prayer requests

Date

Date

Date

Just Different

Is it difficult for you not to cast judgment on someone else's lifestyle choices as being good or bad if they are different than yours? It goes a long way if you can decide instead if that person's choices are complementary to yours, and if they are not, accept their decision to live as they please—absent of your presence. It's ok to be different.

If the person behaves in a way that is offensive or disrespectful to you, you can accept that those behaviors are rooted in the person they are right now, forgive the offense, and disengage. Then continue on your path. If someone has actually sinned against you, confront them with love privately. If your issue is merely a difference in lifestyle choice, you can again accept that they hold beliefs that are different, and without judgment, choose to move forward. However, our main objective as believers is to love others without criticism or condemnation (judgment) to the glory of God.

This week, think about how you can choose to accept differences in other people and either embrace them as they are (if they never change), or release them with love and move forward. Is there someone in your life that you have been judging in an unloving way? Submit them to God. Ask him to show you how best to love them and then be open and ready to do as he leads.

There will be tribulation and distress for every human being who does evil, the Jew first and also the Greek, but glory and honor and peace for everyone who does good, the Jew first and also the Greek. For God shows no partiality.

Romans 2:9-11 ESV

Reflection

Take a moment to get clear about what this week's devotion is saying to you.
Then write how God is leading you to apply it or seek his will.

How I feel God leading me in this area.

_____

_____

_____

_____

The challenges I have faced in this regard.

_____

_____

_____

_____

How I intend to address those challenges as I progress in prayer.

_____

_____

_____

_____

Positive affirmation

This week I declare I am...

I'm grateful for...

What I intend to do...

Affirmation to speak over myself

Prayer requests

Date

Date

Date

Bless with Love

When you come across people who don't have the same values as you do, you can choose not to spend time with them. You don't need to judge, criticize, or condemn them. There's no need to talk about how they behave after you walk away. Simply bless them with love as you leave and continue on your path. If they ask to keep engaging or connecting, kindly decline without the need for an explanation. You selflessly love them in that way. As you release them with a blessing, allow for the possibility of encountering a changed version of them in the future.

If you resist people with judgment, criticism, or condemnation because of their behavior, or bully them into change, you are not loving them. It could be argued that you are also not loving yourself or upholding your internal standard to reflect the character of God by accepting them as they are, and simply disengaging uncomplimentary beliefs and behavior with love.

This week, remember that God is a god of compassion and forgiveness. He holds no record of offense. You don't have to criticize someone whose behavior is contrary to the standards in which you live your life. With compassion, accept that people are who they are. They should still be loved and valued.

> "No! Love your enemies and do good to them; lend and expect nothing back. You will then have a great reward, and you will be children of the Most High God. For he is good to the ungrateful and the wicked. 36Be merciful just as your Father is merciful."
>
> LUKE 6:35-36

Reflection

Take a moment to get clear about what this week's devotion is saying to you.
Then write how God is leading you to apply it or seek his will.

How I feel God leading me in this area.

The challenges I have faced in this regard.

How I intend to address those challenges as I progress in prayer.

Positive affirmation

This week I declare I am...

I'm grateful for...

What I intend to do...

Affirmation to speak over myself

Prayer requests

Date

Date

Date

Willingly

There are two ways to obey God—willingly and unwillingly. The blessing comes when you serve or give willingly and not grudgingly or out of necessity. God loves a cheerful giver, and that doesn't just apply to money. You can't sincerely pray goodwill toward someone you are harboring bitterness toward. Nor can you willingly, with an open heart, obey God if you are rebelling against him in favor of your own desires.

Surrender your will to his way. If that is too hard, pray that God will give you a willing heart. Disobeying God is sin, and it only leads to torment, not to mention cutting yourself off from the blessing he is trying to give you through your obedience.

This week, put serious thought into how you can begin to serve with a willing heart if you are not already doing so. What things need to change to help you get excited about obeying God and seeing all that he has planned for you? And if you already are serving, do a spirit check and ask God to show you your heart concerning all the things that have been entrusted to you in this season.

> Thanks be to God that, though you used to be slaves to sin, you have come to obey from your heart the pattern of teaching that has now claimed your allegiance.
>
> ROMANS 6:17 NIV

Reflection

Take a moment to get clear about what this week's devotion is saying to you. Then write how God is leading you to apply it or seek his will.

How I feel God leading me in this area.
....

....

....

....

....

The challenges I have faced in this regard.
....

....

....

....

....

How I intend to address those challenges as I progress in prayer.
....

....

....

....

....

Positive affirmation

This week I declare I am...

I'm grateful for...

....

....

....

....

What I intend to do...

....

....

....

....

Affirmation to speak over myself

Prayer requests

Date

Date

Date

Hidden Truth

Have you ever done something to someone, or believed something to be a fact, only to later realize your offense or that you were wrong. Sometimes it takes days, months, or even years to recognize. Allow this feeling to drive you to God's Word for better understanding. You may think you were justified in your attitude or behavior toward someone, but it's never okay to be disrespectful no matter what they have done (or you think they have done) to you.

If someone walked up to you and spat in your face, does it mean you forgive them and immediately invite them to go have coffee? No! It means you accept the truth of their actions, which communicates their inability to walk in love toward you. Then disengage and continue on your path (you can also call the cops and press charges as that is an assault, but I digress). Talk to God about it and let the offense go. It doesn't benefit you to carry that around! You should always consult God first on what you should do in difficult situations. He knows what's best and works all things to the highest good of all involved.

This week, write down what forgiveness would look like in a situation that is still unresolved. Pray for God's mercy, asking that he would open your heart to his will and your offender's eyes to their behavior, and continue on your way.

> Jesus was saying, "Father, forgive them;
> for they do not know what they are doing."
> And they cast lots, dividing His garments among themselves.
>
> LUKE 23:34 NASB

Reflection

Take a moment to get clear about what this week's devotion is saying to you. Then write how God is leading you to apply it or seek his will.

How I feel God leading me in this area.

....

....

....

....

The challenges I have faced in this regard.

....

....

....

....

How I intend to address those challenges as I progress in prayer.

....

....

....

....

Positive affirmation

This week I declare I am...

I'm grateful for...

What I intend to do...

Affirmation to speak over myself

Prayer requests

Date

Date

Date

When to Reconnect

When the slate is wiped clean with someone who has hurt you in the past, you don't automatically engage with them, just as you wouldn't engage a stranger. To resume communication and fellowship, they must consistently demonstrate their ability to walk in love toward you. Even if that happens, you have to evaluate if the morals, principles, and beliefs by which you both live are complementary before deciding to reconnect on a consistent basis. Being led by the Holy Spirit will allow you to do this successfully every time.

Whether you decide to engage and connect or not, you will have truly forgiven someone by absolving them of their offense and refusing to hold it against them. Salute the divinity in them. Look at them as God sees them: perfect and made in his image. Bless the past with love and release them. This will result in freedom for both of you.

This week, resolve to be led by the Spirit in everything you do, especially concerning how to walk in love toward others. This starts by asking God to show you how to forgive in a way that is real and lasting to you: not just toward others but also yourself—in the way that God has already forgiven you.

> Get rid of all bitterness, rage and anger, brawling and slander, along with every form of malice. Be kind and compassionate to one another, forgiving each other, just as in Christ God forgave you.
>
> EPHESIANS 4:31-32 NIV

Reflection

Take a moment to get clear about what this week's devotion is saying to you. Then write how God is leading you to apply it or seek his will.

How I feel God leading me in this area.

The challenges I have faced in this regard.

How I intend to address those challenges as I progress in prayer.

Positive affirmation

This week I declare I am...

I'm grateful for...

....

....

....

....

What I intend to do...

....

....

....

....

Affirmation to speak over myself

Prayer requests

Date

Date

Date

Immune to Resentment

You can remain calm in any situation and be immune to resentment. Build your poise upon a rock—Christ within. Call on the law of forgiveness by forgiving any offense and quickly letting it go. Bless the past with love and let it go. Release those who have hurt you and experience the freedom that comes as a result.

Yesterday is gone, and the only things you want to save are those that are good, true, and of real love. Those are the only things that can live in your heart and give life to your soul, thereby restoring it to its God state. All things of material and negative nature, fear, bitterness, and resentment must be left behind. And it is so!

This week, whenever thoughts of past sin and offense come to mind, affirm—out loud—that you and your offender are both free. "I bless you with love and I release you. You are free, and I am free!" True freedom and immunity to resentment is found in divine forgiveness.

"Take heed to yourselves. If your brother sins against you, rebuke him; and if he repents, forgive him. And if he sins against you seven times in a day, and seven times in a day returns to you, saying, 'I repent,' you shall forgive him."

LUKE 17:3-4 NKJV

Reflection

Take a moment to get clear about what this week's devotion is saying to you. Then write how God is leading you to apply it or seek his will.

How I feel God leading me in this area.

....

....

....

....

The challenges I have faced in this regard.

....

....

....

....

How I intend to address those challenges as I progress in prayer.

....

....

....

....

Positive affirmation

This week I declare I am...

I'm grateful for...

What I intend to do...

Affirmation to speak over myself

Prayer requests

Date

Date

Date

A Giving Heart

There is no curse or great consequence that will befall you if you do not give. It is your choice to tithe a tenth, half, nothing at all, or a free will offering of whatever amount. However, the blessings that accompany tithing from a cheerful heart will apply if you do. When you commit in your heart to give toward the work of God in appreciation for his protection, provision, and peace, you **will** be blessed.

If you have been struggling to understand or grudgingly give of your finances, be it toward ministry, a cause, or someone God is calling you to bless, be released from that burden to give freely. Receive God's grace concerning your finances. He will see and reward your desire to give back to him. Perhaps your finances will increase, opportunities for debts to be cleared will surface, contractual obligations may be voided, and various properties might be legally acquired with no financial reserves. He is certainly able to do all of that. Continue to give as God leads. Give and it will be given to you.

This week, meditate on God's history as a provider. Understand that God is your instant, constant, and abundant supply. Be a sower with ample seeds to sow, not just in your finances but in other areas too! Ask God to reveal your resources and get ready to sow. You are blessed to be a blessing in every way including gifts, talents, abilities, and treasures. And it is so!

> Whoever sows sparingly will also reap sparingly, and whoever sows generously will also reap generously. Each of you should give what you have decided in your heart to give, not reluctantly or under compulsion, for God loves a cheerful giver. And God is able to bless you abundantly, so that in all things at all times, having all that you need, you will abound in every good work.
>
> 2 CORINTHIANS 9:6-8 NIV

Reflection

Take a moment to get clear about what this week's devotion is saying to you. Then write how God is leading you to apply it or seek his will.

How I feel God leading me in this area.

The challenges I have faced in this regard.

How I intend to address those challenges as I progress in prayer.

Positive affirmation

This week I declare I am...

I'm grateful for...

What I intend to do...

Affirmation to speak over myself

Prayer requests

Date

Date

Date

Abundant Life in Christ

Why do some people get healed and others don't? Is it a matter of faith, sin, God's perfect will, or a combination of them all? The reality is that no one except God knows the answer. Some believers stake their claim on 1 Peter 2:24, thinking they are guaranteed healing; however, the simple fact that the word states that Christ "bore our sins" on the cross that we might die to sin and live for righteousness denotes that Christ's death provided those who believe with the *spiritual* healing of their sinful condition, not a promise of never-ending physical health.

In accepting God's free gift of salvation, you are given an opportunity for abundant life. No weapon formed against you will prosper, and God will cause all things to work together for your good. But it is also appointed that each person will die at some point unless it is time for Jesus' return. All will experience sickness and pain. What sets you apart from the unbeliever is that while you are awaiting healing, you can choose to thrive and prosper in your thinking, your spirit, and your physical disposition if you continue to speak life and believe in God's power. God can do the impossible!

This week, regardless of any symptoms your body may present, or the report of a physician, choose to speak wholeness and wellness over your body. Rest in the promise that God will work everything, including your affliction, together for your good. And it is so.

> He Himself brought our sins in His body up on the cross,
> so that we might die to sin and live for righteousness;
> by His wounds you were healed.
>
> 1 PETER 2:24 NASB

Reflection

Take a moment to get clear about what this week's devotion is saying to you. Then write how God is leading you to apply it or seek his will.

How I feel God leading me in this area.

The challenges I have faced in this regard.

How I intend to address those challenges as I progress in prayer.

Positive affirmation

This week I declare I am...

I'm grateful for...

What I intend to do...

Affirmation to speak over myself

Prayer requests

Date

Date

Date

Doing the Impossible

God is able to do the impossible. As you rest in his promises and walk in obedience to his Word, giving thanks for everything, you will be kept in perfect peace. He will manifest his strength within you to full perfection while supplying you with enough grace to endure any illness. The first place to look when you are afflicted is within. Go to the Father and ask him to open the eyes of your understanding to anything you may be doing to perpetuate the illness. Sometimes harboring bitterness, anger, unforgiveness, or engaging in perpetual sin can cause affliction.

You can also attract illness by harboring self-defeating thoughts and speaking abusive words. Some diseases could be totally eliminated by forgiving, releasing control, repenting of sinful behavior, or letting go of anger, bitterness, or any other negative emotion concerning a person or situation. You can't harbor positive and negative thoughts simultaneously. It takes extra effort to speak healing and wholeness regardless of how you feel.

This week, instead of speaking negative words about your situation, believe that God is intervening on your behalf to bring you into a state of total and complete wholeness. Pray over yourself daily. Offer a prayer of thanksgiving in anticipation of your healing manifestation. God **is** working on your behalf, so claim it, believe it, and watch him work! And it is so!

Is anyone among you sick? Let them call the elders of the church to pray over them and anoint them with oil in the name of the Lord. And the prayer offered in faith will make the sick person well; the Lord will raise them up. If they have sinned, they will be forgiven.

JAMES 5:14-15 NIV

Reflection

Take a moment to get clear about what this week's devotion is saying to you. Then write how God is leading you to apply it or seek his will.

How I feel God leading me in this area.

The challenges I have faced in this regard.

How I intend to address those challenges as I progress in prayer.

Positive affirmation

This week I declare I am...

I'm grateful for...

What I intend to do...

Affirmation to speak over myself

Prayer requests

Date

Date

Date

While You Wait

Choosing to speak life-affirming words doesn't mean that instant healing will manifest or that there will be no sign of illness. It might bring about treatments to manage the symptoms or enable you to live symptom-free the rest of your life. It may manifest total and complete healing, or help you to stand as your symptoms fade, or aid in extending your life six months or six years longer than the doctor estimated. In the meantime, you can be an example of God's supernatural grace, mercy, and power working through you as you endure. Regardless of the outcome, what you cannot do is continue to speak that you have whatever the illness is. Instead, say that you are daily overcoming the symptoms and believing God for the full manifestation of your healing.

If God told you all that would happen in the course of your healing, would you still rest in the truth that he would provide you with everything you need to endure and have peace while you waited? Would you boldly believe him? Whenever you are afflicted, regardless of the why, choose to speak life, meaning the Word of God, concerning his power and your ability to receive his grace and mercy while you endure.

This week, as you stand in anticipation of total healing for yourself or someone else, bring your illness to God and ask him to reveal if there is anything for you (or them) to do, and if so, how to proceed. While you wait, continue to thank him for comfort, wisdom, and supernatural joy. Believe that he allows things to happen for his purpose, and it will be used for his glory, your good, and the good of others—until the fullness of your healing manifests. And it is so!

> The Lord will sustain him upon his sickbed;
> In his illness, You restore him to health.
>
> PSALM 41:3 NASB

Reflection

Take a moment to get clear about what this week's devotion is saying to you. Then write how God is leading you to apply it or seek his will.

How I feel God leading me in this area.

The challenges I have faced in this regard.

How I intend to address those challenges as I progress in prayer.

Positive affirmation

This week I declare I am...

I'm grateful for...

What I intend to do...

Affirmation to speak over myself

Prayer requests

Date

Date

Date

Loving God and Yourself

What does it mean to love God with all your heart, soul, mind, and strength, and then to love yourself? To love God is to trust and obey him and not your understanding or the world's. It is to walk in total surrender to his will and way for your life, in full assurance of his ability to cover, sustain, and prosper you in the plan he established for your life before time began.

To love yourself is to understand that you are worthy and valuable simply because God created you in his image and classified you as royalty upon completion. Therefore, you live a lifestyle that aligns itself with that understanding, by holding true to the morals, principles, and values befitting royalty! Until you have a thorough understanding of your value and worth from an internal place, you will be at the mercy of external circumstances and forces that anchor your identity.

This week, study the following Scriptures to gain a better understanding of your identity founded on the truth of God's Word. Meditate and internalize them for a deeper understanding of why you are worthy and valuable without external factors. (Read Genesis 1:26–27; Isaiah 43:1; John 1:12–13; Romans 8:31–39; 2 Corinthians 5:17-21; 6:17–18.)

> "'You shall love the Lord your God with all your heart and with all your soul and with all your mind and with all your strength.' The second is this: 'You shall love your neighbor as yourself.' There is no other commandment greater than these."
>
> MARK 12:30-31 ESV

Reflection

Take a moment to get clear about what this week's devotion is saying to you. Then write how God is leading you to apply it or seek his will.

How I feel God leading me in this area.

The challenges I have faced in this regard.

How I intend to address those challenges as I progress in prayer.

Positive affirmation

This week I declare I am...

I'm grateful for...

What I intend to do...

Affirmation to speak over myself

Prayer requests

Date

Date

Date

Fearless Love

Raise your hand if you've ever been hurt by someone you would have never imagined. Now raise your other hand if you've found it difficult to trust again because the magnitude of that hurt was so great that it doesn't seem to fade no matter what you do. Under those circumstances, it might seem fair and logical to protect yourself from further damage. But the truth is that carrying around past hurts only prevents you from moving forward into new, meaningful relationships. It does so by causing you to be fearful of being hurt again, while simultaneously blocking you from receiving the love that a well-meaning person may be looking to give.

God loves you and wants the best for you, including healthy and loving relationships. Besides, it was he who said it is "not good for man to be alone." Therefore, you can start to love *and* trust again when you decide to give your hurt to God and open your heart to the divine connections he intended for you to have.

This week, acknowledge and write down a past hurt you've experienced and have been holding on to. Submit that hurt to God and ask him to heal your heart, by opening the eyes of your understanding to his will concerning that relationship. Then, rest in his ability to bring restoration, and thank him for giving you the courage to love again as he loves—without fear.

> "There is no fear in love, but perfect love casts out fear.
> For fear has to do with punishment,
> and whoever fears has not been perfected in love."
>
> 1 JOHN 4:18

Reflection

Take a moment to get clear about what this week's devotion is saying to you. Then write how God is leading you to apply it or seek his will.

How I feel God leading me in this area.

The challenges I have faced in this regard.

How I intend to address those challenges as I progress in prayer.

Positive affirmation

This week I declare I am...

I'm grateful for...

What I intend to do...

Affirmation to speak over myself

Prayer requests

Date

Date

Date

Divine Connections

This day could start a new day for you in the journey toward God's blessings for your life. Ask him to reveal to you all the connections in your life that are not a part of his plan for you. Then recognize that evil and toxic connections that are not there for good but for harm can be severed in Jesus' name. The family, friend, business, and spiritual connections you have should only be the connections God has for you. Ask him to reveal anyone and anything you need to let go of and submit everything to him.

As you pray about this and depend on God, he will give you the grace, courage, and wisdom to follow through with severing ties and bringing relationships to a close where necessary. In many cases, the person or situation may leave you before you have the chance. Then, ask him to open doors for new, divine connections in your personal, business, and ministry life. Trust him to make choices for you that are for your benefit. And let it be so!

This week, start thanking God for moving you into his purpose and blessing for your life. Ask him to provide the divine connections that benefit you and bring glory to him. He can open doors no one can shut and shut doors no one can open. Watch him do it!

> Do not be unequally yoked with unbelievers.
> For what partnership has righteousness with lawlessness?
> Or what fellowship has light with darkness?
>
> 2 Corinthians 6:14 esv

Reflection

Take a moment to get clear about what this week's devotion is saying to you. Then write how God is leading you to apply it or seek his will.

How I feel God leading me in this area. ....

....

....

....

....

The challenges I have faced in this regard. ....

....

....

....

....

How I intend to address those challenges as I progress in prayer. ....

....

....

....

....

Positive affirmation

This week I declare I am...

I'm grateful for...

What I intend to do...

Affirmation to speak over myself

Prayer requests

Date

Date

Date

Loving God

How can you walk in love toward God? You may have been given all kinds of both direct and indirect instructions on how to follow God (i.e. how to be a "good Christian"). Sometimes this leads to a belief that God is waiting to crack you over the head with a spiritual baseball bat at every offense. And as a result, he may feel like an invisible, intangible, unreal reality in your everyday existence. How could you truly love someone like that?

The answer is in God's Word! You can go directly there and find his very clear instruction. He promises that his Holy Spirit will lead and guide you into all truth, teaching you *all* things. Emulating the speech and mannerisms of your pastor, leaders, or other seasoned saints in an attempt to find what your walk of faith should look like will eventually leave you feeling dissatisfied. Consulting spiritual leaders for insight is one thing, but searching the Scriptures for yourself is both commendable and beneficial. Let the Holy Spirit guide you today.

Everyone's life, path, and purpose is tailor-made by God for them. This week, ask God for instruction on how you should navigate the path he is assigning you. He has given you a unique set of gifts, talents, and abilities for his purpose, and he is committed to working in and through your for his glory.

> "Whoever has my commands and keeps them is the one who loves me. The one who loves me will be loved by my Father, and I too will love them and show myself to them."
>
> JOHN 14:21 NIV

Reflection

Take a moment to get clear about what this week's devotion is saying to you. Then write how God is leading you to apply it or seek his will.

How I feel God leading me in this area.

....

....

....

....

The challenges I have faced in this regard.

....

....

....

....

How I intend to address those challenges as I progress in prayer.

....

....

....

....

Positive affirmation

This week I declare I am...

I'm grateful for...

What I intend to do...

Affirmation to speak over myself

Prayer requests

Date

Date

Date

Deeper Connection

Take time to meditate on Scriptures that speak about how you can walk in love toward God and others. Surrender your heart to the Father daily, asking him to empower you through the Holy Spirit, so you can live out his Word. You cannot walk your walk of faith without him! How can you love someone you don't know?

In your daily prayer time, ask the Father to reveal himself to you. He can teach you how to live out his Word as you strive to memorize it, planting it deep in your heart and rooting it way down in your soul. Then you can open your heart to receive what God has for your life, not in the way you want or think or feel, but in gratitude with expectation. He will make it unequivocally known, ordering your steps and making your path straight. His love for you will be clear and evident to all. And so it is!

This week, ask God to take you into a deeper, more meaningful relationship with him where you will grow in faith and hear his still small voice within your soul. Surrender your being to his will, acknowledging how much you need him while thanking him for his many blessings in your life.

> "Keep this Book of the Law always on your lips; meditate on it day and night, so that you may be careful to do everything written in it. Then you will be prosperous and successful."
>
> JOSHUA 1:8 NIV

Reflection

Take a moment to get clear about what this week's devotion is saying to you. Then write how God is leading you to apply it or seek his will.

How I feel God leading me in this area.

....

....

....

....

The challenges I have faced in this regard.

....

....

....

....

How I intend to address those challenges as I progress in prayer.

....

....

....

....

Positive affirmation

This week I declare I am...

I'm grateful for...

What I intend to do...

Affirmation to speak over myself

Date

Date

Date

Affirming Divine Love

Divine love can dissolve and dissipate every wrong condition in your mind, body, and affairs. It is the most powerful chemical in the universe, and it dissolves everything that is not of itself. There is nothing without divine love.

If you keep God's Word, his love has been perfected in you. This is how you can know that you are in him: if you say you abide in him, then you will walk like Jesus walked. You must believe that you are beautiful and worthy of love. Allow your heart to be ready and open. As a richly illuminated child of God, filled with divine love and wisdom, you can be led into that which is for your highest good. When you love the best in all people, you will draw the highest and best people to yourself for your mutual good and blessing. Allow God's love and harmony to be at work in your relationships. Welcome love with open arms.

Are you grateful for the abundance of love in your life? This week, think about ways you can naturally attract love in your life everywhere you go. Start by loving God and yourself deeply and with passion today!

> "There is no fear in love. But perfect love drives out fear, because fear has to do with punishment. The one who fears is not made perfect in love."
>
> 1 JOHN 4:18 NIV

Reflection

Take a moment to get clear about what this week's devotion is saying to you. Then write how God is leading you to apply it or seek his will.

How I feel God leading me in this area.

The challenges I have faced in this regard.

How I intend to address those challenges as I progress in prayer.

Positive affirmation

This week I declare I am...

I'm grateful for...

What I intend to do...

Affirmation to speak over myself

Prayer requests

Date

Date

Date

Loving Your Neighbor

It is easy to love people who are nice, kind, welcoming, and whom you consider to have a good heart. The same may not be true for those who are rude, selfish, unkind, or abrasive. Like any problem, it would seem the easiest way to deal with these people is to just let them be. Unfortunately, resolving to handle them in any way other than with love leaves you open to be treated with that same fate.

You condemn yourself to the same judgment when you criticize your neighbor for their unacceptable behavior and then banish them with condemnation. No one but God is in the position to do that. Depending on the lens through which others view life, it is guaranteed that someone will find displeasure in you at some point. Whether it's right or wrong, just or unjust, one day someone will have an issue with your looks, attitude, behavior, status, or sometimes, quite simply, your presence. Love is the only way to successfully navigate that tough path.

Whether accusations are rational or completely unfounded, you are called to walk in love toward your neighbor. This week, especially during times of conflict, think about and write down ways you can show love to "difficult" people to the glory of God.

"If you love those who love you, what credit is that to you? Even sinners love those who love them. But love your enemies, do good to them, and lend to them without expecting to get anything back. Then your reward will be great, and you will be children of the Most High, because he is kind to the ungrateful and wicked."

LUKE 6:32-35 NIV

Reflection

Take a moment to get clear about what this week's devotion is saying to you. Then write how God is leading you to apply it or seek his will.

How I feel God leading me in this area.

....

....

....

....

The challenges I have faced in this regard.

....

....

....

....

How I intend to address those challenges as I progress in prayer.

....

....

....

....

Positive affirmation

This week I declare I am...

I'm grateful for...

What I intend to do...

Affirmation to speak over myself

Prayer requests

Date

Date

Date

Lasting Transformation

All believers are called to walk in love toward their neighbors—not just their Christian brothers and sisters, but also those who don't look, walk, talk, think, or believe as they do. The reality is that it is not possible to do this with any consistency without the assistance of the Holy Spirit, working in tandem with both a renewed mind and spirit.

Salvation takes care of the conversion required to provide you with a new heart and new spirit. However, transformation comes when you renew your mind through God's Word, meaning memorizing it, speaking it, praying it, and asking God to show you how to apply it to your life on a daily basis. Speaking the Word of God often throughout the day is required to effectuate lasting transformation in your life. Humans are prone to looking for comfort, convenience, and safety. Doing something easy is preferred over tackling difficulty. And change is not always easy; sometimes it's downright hard, and the process can take days, weeks, or even years.

This week, take a moment to review a few of your notes from prior weeks. Specifically concerning areas of difficulty—forgiveness, unbelief, conflict, etc.— and strengthen your resolve to align your will with God's will in those areas. Then, affirm out loud any reference affirmations or Scriptures you noted and believe that lasting change and transformation will continue to manifest as you continue to surrender yourself to God's will.

> "Do not conform to the pattern of this world, but be transformed by the renewing of your mind. Then you will be able to test and approve what God's will is—his good, pleasing and perfect will."
>
> ROMANS 12:2 NIV

Reflection

Take a moment to get clear about what this week's devotion is saying to you.
Then write how God is leading you to apply it or seek his will.

How I feel God leading me in this area.

....

....

....

....

The challenges I have faced in this regard.

....

....

....

....

How I intend to address those challenges as I progress in prayer.

....

....

....

....

Positive affirmation

This week I declare I am...

I'm grateful for...

What I intend to do...

Affirmation to speak over myself

Prayer requests

Date

Date

Date

Choosing Love

God's Word commands us to love. When it comes to loving those you deem unlovable or unworthy of your love, that command doesn't change. So how do you love someone who has proven themselves to be incapable of honoring the divinity in you, or reciprocating the love and respect you aspire to give? You love others as you love yourself. That means you accept them as they are, in respect to who you are and the standard by which you've been called by God to live your life. If you don't know who you are in God and do not love yourself enough to uphold a righteous standard, regardless of the external influence suggesting otherwise, loving the unlovable is impossible.

When you commit to seeing others as God sees them, you choose to walk in gratitude and away from criticism and judgment. You don't try to change people or demand that they get in line and do things your way. As you pursue divine love, you will find yourself showing more grace and compassion than you ever deemed possible.

This week, surrender yourself to God's will concerning how to love your neighbors. Take note of the peace and freedom that comes with accepting people as they are without criticism or condemnation. This is how God loves you.

> "'Love the Lord your God with all your heart and with all your soul and with all your mind and with all your strength.' The second is this: 'Love your neighbor as yourself.' There is no commandment greater than these."
>
> MARK 12:30-31 NIV

Reflection

Take a moment to get clear about what this week's devotion is saying to you. Then write how God is leading you to apply it or seek his will.

How I feel God leading me in this area.

The challenges I have faced in this regard.

How I intend to address those challenges as I progress in prayer.

Positive affirmation

This week I declare I am...

I'm grateful for...

What I intend to do...

Affirmation to speak over myself

Prayer requests

Date

Date

Date

The Whole Armor

The Word of God provides you with the necessary tools required to stand against the enemy as God fights your battles. Do you let him fight for you, or is the armor just there for show? Don't wait until you've done everything you can think of before calling on God to help! Instead, start each day by dressing yourself in the equipment provided, acknowledging your need for God to war against the enemy as you protect your mind, heart, and assignment with his divine armor.

Pray on your armor and endeavor to activate each piece through speaking and applying God's Word in every situation. As with anything you desire to last in life, first acknowledge that desire through your spoken commitment. Then carry out the commitment with consistent action.

You cannot live your life as a believer alone. You need God's help. This week, start your day with prayer by acknowledging the armor your Father has provided and activating it through the practice of affirming his Word. Read Ephesians 6:13-18 out loud and practice memorizing this crucial Scripture for future use.

Put on the full armor of God, so that when the day of evil comes, you may be able to stand your ground, and after you have done everything, to stand. Stand firm then, with the belt of truth buckled around your waist, with the breastplate of righteousness in place, and with your feet fitted with the readiness that comes from the gospel of peace. In addition to all this, take up the shield of faith, with which you can extinguish all the flaming arrows of the evil one. Take the helmet of salvation and the sword of the Spirit, which is the word of God.

EPHESIANS 6:13-18 NIV

Reflection

Take a moment to get clear about what this week's devotion is saying to you. Then write how God is leading you to apply it or seek his will.

How I feel God leading me in this area.

The challenges I have faced in this regard.

How I intend to address those challenges as I progress in prayer.

Positive affirmation

This week I declare I am...

I'm grateful for...

What I intend to do...

Affirmation to speak over myself

Prayer requests

Date

Date

Date

Each Piece Matters

The enemy can't put his hands on you. Take up the whole armor of God, that he provided to help you stand, and resist the enemy until he flees. He *will* flee because God's Word promises he will when you resist him, and that requires making sure you are wearing the right armor!

Last week's devotional stated our spiritual armor as explained in Ephesians 6. Let's start off this week by thanking God for each piece of the armor he has given you. Your war is not against flesh and blood, so stand firm with the belt of truth buckled around your waist. God's Word is truth, and every decision you make should be based on it. Put the breastplate of righteousness on so your heart is protected. Fit your feet with the readiness that comes from the gospel of peace. The shield of faith will help you extinguish the flaming arrows of the evil one. With the helmet of salvation, you can protect your mind, thoughts, dreams, vision, and everything you look at. The sword of the Spirit, which is the Word of God, gives you the Scriptures you need to speak against the enemy when he comes to attack you. Stand strong in Jesus' name and by the power of the Holy Spirit!

God has equipped you with the armor you need for every task you are called to. Truth, righteousness, peace, faith, salvation, and the Word of God are the weapons that will ensure your victory. Be intentional about taking them up every day.

> He gives more grace. Therefore it says: "God opposes the proud, but gives grace to the humble." Submit yourselves therefore to God. Resist the devil, and he will flee from you. Draw near to God, and he will draw near to you."
>
> JAMES 4:6-8 ESV

Reflection

Take a moment to get clear about what this week's devotion is saying to you. Then write how God is leading you to apply it or seek his will.

How I feel God leading me in this area.

....

....

....

....

The challenges I have faced in this regard.

....

....

....

....

How I intend to address those challenges as I progress in prayer.

....

....

....

....

Positive affirmation

This week I declare I am...

I'm grateful for...

What I intend to do...

Affirmation to speak over myself

Prayer requests

Date

Date

Date

Losing to Find

How do you know that the person you are is the highest expression of your true self, and the purpose you are walking in was unequivocally laid by God? The truth is that you can't until you have undergone the process of laying yourself and your plans on his altar for searching. Coming into the knowledge of your self-worth in God is dependent on you surrendering to his process.

Your value is assigned to you the moment God created you. Until you go before the Father to learn of your divine identity and subsequent purpose in him, the person you present to the world will be a construct of your own imagination, and everything you produce will be subject to limitations. If you seek to save your life, you will lose it. But if you lose your life for the cause of Christ, you will find it. More plainly said, if you give up your time, talent, and treasure for the things of God, you will truly find your life.

This week, if you haven't already done so, take a moment and submit at least one plan you've been pondering to God. Ask him to show you his will concerning it, and how you should proceed if it is his will. Then patiently wait for his leading.

> "If anyone wants to come after Me, he must deny himself, take up his cross, and follow Me. For whoever wants to save his life will lose it; but whoever loses his life for My sake will find it."
>
> MATTHEW 16:24-25 NASB

Reflection

Take a moment to get clear about what this week's devotion is saying to you.
Then write how God is leading you to apply it or seek his will.

How I feel God leading me in this area.

The challenges I have faced in this regard.

How I intend to address those challenges as I progress in prayer.

Positive affirmation

This week I declare I am...

I'm grateful for...

What I intend to do...

Affirmation to speak over myself

Prayer requests

Date

Date

Date

Divine Surrender

How can you lose your soul while pursuing your own life? You surrender yourself to things that draw you away from God's perfect plan, and you become someone he didn't intend for you to be. You might not even recognize yourself anymore. Dreams and visions you once had may seem empty even if already recognized.

You must understand the necessity of placing yourself before the Father to understand his blueprint concerning all things *you* before you take another step in life. If it turns out that you are completely off course and everything must be blown to bits in order to set things straight, it's better that happens sooner than later. God promised to work everything out for your good, which includes the consequences of selfish decisions made in pursuit of your own self-interests.

This week, place yourself before God for his take on your life's vision. Meditate on what he shows you and be sure to write it down as you prepare to follow his leading. Otherwise, you will always be guessing, proving, and striving to be someone and do something he may not have called you to be and do.

> "What good will it do a person if he gains the whole world,
> but forfeits his soul? Or what will a person give in exchange for his soul?"
>
> MATTHEW 16:26 NASB

Reflection

Take a moment to get clear about what this week's devotion is saying to you. Then write how God is leading you to apply it or seek his will.

How I feel God leading me in this area.

....

....

....

....

The challenges I have faced in this regard.

....

....

....

....

How I intend to address those challenges as I progress in prayer.

....

....

....

....

Positive affirmation

This week I declare I am...

I'm grateful for...

What I intend to do...

Affirmation to speak over myself

Prayer requests

Date

Date

Date

Heart Desires

You were created with a unique set of characteristics, gifts, talents, and abilities that were given to you to fulfill God's divine purpose, crafted specifically for you. The desires spoken of in Psalm 37:4 are the desires *God* places there.

As you surrender your will and way to God, you may begin to desire some things that you never thought about or even saw growing up. You may have no idea why you now want things that you either never wanted, were totally against, or never appeared to be obtainable. As you delight yourself in the Lord, you will have a boldness about pursuing the desires that God places on your heart, and your biggest desire will be to live a life that glorifies him in every way.

This week, take a moment to write down some of the desires God has placed in your heart. Then submit them to God in full assurance that he is more than able to manifest those desires for your good and his glory!

> Delight yourself also in the Lord,
> And He shall give you the desires of your heart.
>
> PSALM 37:4 NKJV

Reflection

Take a moment to get clear about what this week's devotion is saying to you. Then write how God is leading you to apply it or seek his will.

How I feel God leading me in this area.

....

....

....

....

The challenges I have faced in this regard.

....

....

....

....

How I intend to address those challenges as I progress in prayer.

....

....

....

....

Positive affirmation

This week I declare I am...

I'm grateful for...

What I intend to do...

Affirmation to speak over myself

Prayer requests

Date

Date

Date

More than Once

Divine surrender is not a one-time event. You must submit yourself to God daily, acknowledging your need to lay your heart before him in submission to his will, in total dependence on him. In doing so, you affirm that it is not your will but his will, not your way but his way, and not your time but his time. Doing this as part of your daily spiritual practice invites God to take a front-row seat in your life. It also prevents your carnal mind from rising up and taking the lead on decisions concerning challenges, opportunities, and ideas that must be brought before the throne of God for his input.

Like an organ transplant patient takes anti-rejection drugs to ensure their new organ works efficiently in their old body, a spiritual heart transplant requires taking spiritual anti-rejection medication, by seeking God's input on everything—daily—through prayer, Bible study, and speaking his Word.

Start out this week by declaring that your will, your way, and your time is surrendered to God. Then ask him to show you how he would like you to proceed. Yes, you have your routine, but acknowledge your willingness to change your plans if at any time the Lord leads.

> Humble yourselves, therefore, under the mighty hand of God so that at the proper time he may exalt you, casting all your anxieties on him, because he cares for you.
>
> 1 Peter 5:6-7 esv

Reflection

Take a moment to get clear about what this week's devotion is saying to you. Then write how God is leading you to apply it or seek his will.

How I feel God leading me in this area. ....

....

....

....

....

The challenges I have faced in this regard. ....

....

....

....

....

How I intend to address those challenges as I progress in prayer. ....

....

....

....

....

Positive affirmation

This week I declare I am...

I'm grateful for...

What I intend to do...

Affirmation to speak over myself

Prayer requests

Date

Date

Date

Light Weight

Surrendering yourself might seem like an impossible task, but in reality, all you're being asked to do is give yourself to God. He will do the rest. The taking up of your cross is simply taking up God's purpose for your life, endeavoring to learn of him and live for him in the process.

When you surrender to him, he promises that the weight of what he's called you to do will be light, and your soul will be at rest because it will be operating in harmony with the plan and purpose to which he's called you. You won't be trying to figure out who and how to be when you commit to being who he called you to be.

This week, as you continue along the path of surrender, rest in knowing that because you have surrendered to what God has called you to, your every need and the righteous desires of your heart will be fulfilled. Surrender is simply about acknowledging your resolve to lay down your will in place of the Father's, in exchange for his highest good manifesting in every area of your life. Through a totally surrendered person, God will perform the supernatural!

> "Come to Me, all who are weary and burdened, and I will give you rest. Take My yoke upon you and learn from Me, for I am gentle and humble in heart, and you will find rest for your souls. For My yoke is comfortable, and My burden is light."
>
> MATTHEW 11:28-30 NASB

Reflection

Take a moment to get clear about what this week's devotion is saying to you. Then write how God is leading you to apply it or seek his will.

How I feel God leading me in this area.

_____

_____

_____

The challenges I have faced in this regard.

_____

_____

_____

_____

How I intend to address those challenges as I progress in prayer.

_____

_____

_____

_____

Positive affirmation

This week I declare I am...

I'm grateful for...

What I intend to do...

Affirmation to speak over myself

Prayer requests

Date

Date

Date

Highest Expression

Did you know that God's strength is made perfect in your weakness (when you lay down your will and take up his)? Although he promised that taking on the load of his purpose for your life would be easy, he didn't promise that it would be easy to wait on him when in need, trust in him with all your heart under pressure, and stand up to people and institutions who challenge your resolve to follow him. Thankfully his Word says over and over that all you need to do is stand in his purpose, and he will do all the defending.

Be encouraged to go before God concerning your life. Even if you think you're on track, the only way to know is to formally surrender yourself and your plans for his review. That is how you ensure everything aligns with his preordained marching orders for your life.

The process of surrender is not easy. Many have worked on their life's plan for years! They had it all mapped out and had no intention of changing it. This topic was extended over several weeks to help you gradually lay down your plans and get God's take. Your plans might already align with his; however, even if some of them don't, God's guidance concerning your identify and purpose is guaranteed to produce the highest expression of your divine self in the earth—for his glory, your good, and the good of others. And it is so!

> He said to me, "My grace is sufficient for you, for my power is made perfect in weakness." Therefore I will boast all the more gladly about my weaknesses, so that Christ's power may rest on me.
>
> 2 CORINTHIANS 2:9 NIV

Reflection

Take a moment to get clear about what this week's devotion is saying to you. Then write how God is leading you to apply it or seek his will.

How I feel God leading me in this area.

The challenges I have faced in this regard.

How I intend to address those challenges as I progress in prayer.

Positive affirmation

This week I declare I am...

I'm grateful for...

What I intend to do...

Affirmation to speak over myself

Prayer requests

Date

Date

Date

Divine Self-worth

After you ask God to show you who you are, ask him how you should live according to the standard that befits your royal status. You are the daughter of the King after all! Royalty doesn't just hang out with anyone. It doesn't eat any old thing or go to unsavory places. It has a certain kind of walk, talk, and disposition. It presents a poise that only comes about through a firm grounding in the knowledge of your royal standing and the power that status effectuates in the world. Even the Queen of England had to be groomed. While she was royalty from birth, she still had to be taught how to be *royalty.*

Who else can better teach you how to walk in power, yet quiet strength, grace, poise, and all things royal than the King of Kings and Lord of Lords himself? How do you know that you are loved, valued, and worthy just for who you are not because of your accomplishments, appearance, talents, etc. if you don't know what true inner self-worth is? Where does your identity come from if you haven't been raised to affirm that you are loved and valuable just for being you?

This week, take some time to search God's Word for Scriptures that declare your divine worth in God, like Jeremiah 29:11. That is the best way to internalize an understanding of your incredible worth founded in the simple truth that God created and chose you, and therefore you are both valuable and loved!

> You are a chosen race, a royal priesthood, a holy nation, a people for his own possession, that you may proclaim the excellencies of him who called you out of darkness into his marvelous light.
>
> 1 PETER 2:9 ESV

Reflection

Take a moment to get clear about what this week's devotion is saying to you. Then write how God is leading you to apply it or seek his will.

How I feel God leading me in this area.

_____

_____

_____

_____

The challenges I have faced in this regard.

_____

_____

_____

_____

How I intend to address those challenges as I progress in prayer.

_____

_____

_____

_____

Positive affirmation

This week I declare I am...

I'm grateful for...

What I intend to do...

Affirmation to speak over myself

Prayer requests

Date

Date

Date

Active Power of Stillness

What is it about human nature that compels you to just do something, even when you have no idea what to do? Oftentimes, the first inclination is to act: call someone, make a list of pros and cons, stand up for yourself, and so on. But it only makes things worse.

God is always there waiting for those who trust in him to seek his guidance and instruction, even when the circumstances of life or those closest to you demand that you do something.

This week, be mindful that trusting God is not always about doing. Sometimes stillness is required, allowing you to avoid taking quick action when challenges arise, and place your thoughts before God in prayer. Ask for guidance before acting and see how he shows up in your life when you wait for, receive, and follow his instruction.

> Since ancient times no one has heard,
> no ear has perceived,
> no eye has seen any God besides you,
> who acts on behalf of those who wait for him.
>
> ISAIAH 64:4 NIV

Reflection

Take a moment to get clear about what this week's devotion is saying to you. Then write how God is leading you to apply it or seek his will.

How I feel God leading me in this area.

....

....

....

....

The challenges I have faced in this regard.

....

....

....

....

How I intend to address those challenges as I progress in prayer.

....

....

....

....

Positive affirmation

This week I declare I am...

I'm grateful for...

What I intend to do...

Affirmation to speak over myself

Prayer requests

Date

Date

Date

Pathway to Victory

On any given day, you could probably find at least ten things to complain about. Those problems, circumstances, and feelings are very real, and can drag you into a dark abyss of continuous despair if you let them. There are also several things that are simultaneously going well: things like family or pets that love you, employment, housing, and even a full set of working senses that include the ability to see and enjoy God's creation.

Your disposition raises to the elevation you intentionally aspire it to be, and you get there by maintaining an attitude of gratitude and thanksgiving. This will help you remain in a state of joy while also pleasing the Lord.

This week, make an extra effort to recognize at least two things that are going right whenever something that is going wrong tries to steal your joy. Then, be focused and intentional in your praise as you give thanks for how God is moving on your behalf. He is up to something good, and you should rejoice and be glad about it!

> Through Him then, let's continually offer up a sacrifice of praise to God, that is, the fruit of lips praising His name. And do not neglect doing good and sharing, for with such sacrifices God is pleased.
>
> HEBREWS 13:15-16 NASB

Reflection

Take a moment to get clear about what this week's devotion is saying to you.
Then write how God is leading you to apply it or seek his will.

How I feel God leading me in this area.

....

....

....

....

The challenges I have faced in this regard.

....

....

....

....

How I intend to address those challenges as I progress in prayer.

....

....

....

....

Positive affirmation

This week I declare I am...

I'm grateful for...

What I intend to do...

Affirmation to speak over myself

Prayer requests

Date

Date

Date

The Best Is Yet to Come

Did you know that God really does have a blessing with your name on it? In fact, several have already been dispatched and are on their way to your front door. I'm not just talking about spiritual blessings, but even those tangible blessings that you have been believing him for, both openly and in secret.

It is often not possible to receive and store certain deliveries when there is already something in its place, or you are not fully available to receive them.

This week, take some time to take stock by noting a few things that you need to let go of or "forget." This should go without saying, but these items sometimes include things that are already gone, but you refuse to release. In whatever scenario you may find yourself, ask God to help you let go and forget, so you can make room for what he has coming. God wants the best for you, but you must be willing to open your hand and let go, so you can receive the better of what's gone. And it is so!

> "Forget the former things;
> do not dwell on the past.
> See, I am doing a new thing!
> Now it springs u; do you not perceive it?
> I am making a way in the wilderness
> and streams in the wasteland."
>
> ISAIAH 43:18-19 NIV

Reflection

Take a moment to get clear about what this week's devotion is saying to you. Then write how God is leading you to apply it or seek his will.

How I feel God leading me in this area.

The challenges I have faced in this regard.

How I intend to address those challenges as I progress in prayer.

Positive affirmation

This week I declare I am...

I'm grateful for...

What I intend to do...

Affirmation to speak over myself

Prayer requests

Date

Date

Date

AFFLICTION

He has not despise or abhorred
the affliction of the afflicted,
and he has not hidden his face from him,
but has heard, when he cried to him.
PSALM 22:24 ESV

The afflicted will eat and be satisfied;
Those who seek Him will praise the LORD.
May your heart live forever!
PSALM 22:26 NASB

The afflictions of the righteous are many,
But the LORD rescues him from them all.
PSALM 34:19 NASB

It is good for me that I have
been afflicted,
That I may learn Your
statutes.
PSALM 119:71 NKJV

We do not lose heart.
Though our outer self is
wasting away, our inner self is
being renewed day by day. For this
light momentary affliction is preparing
for us an eternal weight of glory beyond
all comparison, as we look not to the
things that are seen but to the things
that are unseen. For the things that are
seen are transient, but the things that are
unseen are eternal.
2 CORINTHIANS 4:16-18 ESV

My brethren, count it all joy when you
fall into various trials, knowing that the
testing of your faith produces patience.
But let patience have its perfect work,
that you may be perfect and complete,
lacking nothing.
JAMES 1:2-4 NKJV

We also glory in our sufferings, because
we know that suffering produces
perseverance; perseverance, character;
and character, hope. And hope does not
put us to shame, because God's love has
been poured out into our hearts through
the Holy Spirit, who has been given to us.
ROMANS 5:3-5 NIV

ANGER

Fools show their annoyance at once,
but the prudent overlook an insult.
PROVERBS 12:16 NIV

One who is slow to anger has
great understanding;
But one who is quick-
tempered exalts
foolishness.
PROVERBS 14:29 NASB

"Be angry and do not sin":
do not let the sun go down
on your wrath, nor give place
to the devil.
EPHESIANS 4:26-27 NKJV

A soft answer turns away wrath,
But a harsh word stirs up anger.
PROVERBS 15:1 NKJV

A hot-tempered person stirs up conflict,
but the one who is patient calms a
quarrel.
PROVERBS 15:18 NIV

Whoever is slow to anger is better than
the mighty,
and he who rules his spirit than he who
takes a city.
PROVERBS 16:32 ESV

AFFIRM
—THE—
WORD

One who withholds his words has knowledge,
And one who has a cool spirit is a person of understanding.
PROVERBS 17:27 NASB

The discretion of a man makes him slow to anger,
And his glory is to overlook a transgression.
PROVERBS 19:11 NKJV

A fool always loses his temper,
But a wise person holds it back.
PROVERBS 29:11 NASB

Do not be quickly provoked in your spirit, for anger resides in the lap of fools.
ECCLESIASTES 7:9 NIV

Everyone should be quick to listen, slow to speak and slow to become angry, because human anger does not produce the righteousness that God desires.
JAMES 1:19-20 NIV

ANXIETY

"Have I not commanded you? Be strong and courageous. Do not be frightened, and do not be dismayed, for the LORD your God is with you wherever you go."
JOSHUA 1:9 ESV

"For this reason I say to you, do not be worried about your life, as to what you will eat or what you will drink; nor for your body, as to what you will put on. Is life not more than food, and the body more than clothing? Look at the birds of the sky, that they do not sow, nor reap, nor gather crops into barns, and yet your heavenly Father feeds them. Are you not much more important than they? And

which of you by worrying can add a single day to his life's span?
MATTHEW 6:25-27 NASB

Be anxious for nothing, but in everything by prayer and supplication, with thanksgiving, let your requests be made known to God; and the peace of God, which surpasses all understanding, will guard your hearts and minds through Christ Jesus.
PHILIPPIANS 4:6-7 NKJV

"Peace I leave with you; my peace I give to you. Not as the world gives do I give to you. Let not your hearts be troubled, neither let them be afraid.
JOHN 14:27 ESV

ASKING

"Ask and it will be given to you; seek and you will find; knock and the door will be opened to you. For everyone who asks receives; the one who seeks finds; and to the one who knocks, the door will be opened."
MATTHEW 7:7-8 NIV

"I say to you, all things for which you pray and ask, believe that you have received them, and they will be granted to you."
MARK 11:24 NASB

"If you abide in Me, and My words abide in you, you will ask what you desire, and it shall be done for you."
JOHN 15:7 NKJV

Do not be anxious about anything, but in everything by prayer and supplication with thanksgiving let your requests be made known to God. And the peace of God, which surpasses all understanding,

will guard your hearts and your minds in Christ Jesus.
PHILIPPIANS 4:6-7 ESV

This is the confidence which we have before Him, that, if we ask anything according to His will, He hears us. And if we know that He hears us in whatever we ask, we know that we have the requests which we have asked from Him.
1 JOHN 5:14-15 NASB

BELIEF

Jesus said to him, "'If You can?' All things are possible for the one who believes."
MARK 9:23 NASB

"He who believes in Him is not condemned; but he who does not believe is condemned already, because he has not believed in the name of the only begotten Son of God."
JOHN 3:18 NKJV

These are written that you may believe that Jesus is the Messiah, the Son of God, and that by believing you may have life in his name.
JOHN 20:31 NIV

I pray that the eyes of your heart may be enlightened, so that you will know what is the hope of His calling, what are the riches of the glory of His inheritance in the saints, and what is the boundless greatness of His power toward us who believe. These are in accordance with the working of the strength of His might.
EPHESIANS 1:18-19 NASB

Though you have not seen him, you love him; and even though you do not see him now, you believe in him and are filled with an inexpressible and glorious joy, for you are receiving the end result of your faith, the salvation of your souls.
1 PETER 1:8-9 NIV

BLESSINGS

The blessing of the LORD brings wealth, without painful toil for it.
PROVERBS 10:22 NIV

When a man's ways please the LORD, he makes even his enemies to be at peace with him.
PROVERBS 16:7 ESV

"Eye has not seen, nor ear heard, Nor have entered into the heart of man The things which God has prepared for those who love Him."
1 CORINTHIANS 2:9 NKJV

God is able to bless you abundantly, so that in all things at all times, having all that you need, you will abound in every good work.
2 CORINTHIANS 9:8 NIV

Blessed be the God and Father of our Lord Jesus Christ, who has blessed us in Christ with every spiritual blessing in the heavenly places.
EPHESIANS 1:3 ESV

If you are willing and obedient, You will eat the best of the land.
ISAIAH 1:19 NASB

Every good gift and every perfect gift is from above, and comes down from the Father of lights, with whom there is no variation or shadow of turning.
JAMES 1:17 NKJV

BOLDNESS

"Be strong and courageous, and act; do not fear nor be dismayed, for the LORD God, my God, is with you. He will not fail you nor forsake you until all the work for the service of the house of the LORD is finished."
1 CHRONICLES 28:20 NASB

"Have I not commanded you? Be strong and courageous. Do not be afraid; do not be discouraged, for the LORD your God will be with you wherever you go."
JOSHUA 1:9 NIV

Let us then with confidence draw near to the throne of grace, that we may receive mercy and find grace to help in time of need.
HEBREWS 4:16 ESV

I eagerly expect and hope that I will in no way be ashamed, but will have sufficient courage so that now as always Christ will be exalted in my body, whether by life or by death.
PHILIPPIANS 1:20 NIV

Pray in the Spirit on all occasions with all kinds of prayers and requests. With this in mind, be alert and always keep on praying for all the Lord's people. Pray also for me, that whenever I speak, words may be given me so that I will fearlessly make known the mystery of the gospel, for which I am an ambassador in chains. Pray that I may declare it fearlessly, as I should.
EPHESIANS 6:18-20 NIV

The wicked flee when no one pursues, but the righteous are bold as a lion.
PROVERBS 28:1 ESV

COMFORT

You shall increase my greatness,
And comfort me on every side.
PSALM 71:21 NKJV

Even though I walk
through the darkest valley,
I will fear no evil,
for you are with me;
your rod and your staff,
they comfort me.
PSALM 23:4 NIV

"Blessed are those who mourn, for they shall be comforted."
MATTHEW 5:4 ESV

"Come to Me, all who are weary and burdened, and I will give you rest. Take My yoke upon you and learn from Me, for I am gentle and humble in heart, and you will find rest for your souls. For My yoke is comfortable, and My burden is light."
MATTHEW 11:28-30 NASB

I love the LORD, because He has heard My voice and my supplications.
Because He has inclined His ear to me,
Therefore I will call upon Him as long as I live.
PSALM 116:1-2 NKJV

Praise be to the God and Father of our Lord Jesus Christ, the Father of compassion and the God of all comfort, who comforts us in all our troubles, so that we can comfort those in any trouble with the comfort we ourselves receive from God.
2 CORINTHIANS 1:3-4 NIV

CONDEMNATION

Having been justified by faith, we have peace with God through our Lord Jesus Christ.
ROMANS 5:1 NKJV

There is now no condemnation at all for those who are in Christ Jesus. For the law of the Spirit of life in Christ Jesus has set you free from the law of sin and of death. For what the Law could not do, weak as it was through the flesh, God did: sending His own Son in the likeness of sinful flesh and as an offering for sin, He condemned sin in the flesh, so that the requirement of the Law might be fulfilled in us who do not walk according to the flesh but according to the Spirit. For those who are in accord with the flesh set their minds on the things of the flesh, but those who are in accord with the Spirit, the things of the Spirit.
ROMANS 8:1-5 NASB

"Whoever believes in him is not condemned, but whoever does not believe is condemned already, because he has not believed in the name of the only Son of God."
JOHN 3:18 ESV

CONFESSION

One who conceals his wrongdoings will not prosper,
But one who confesses and abandons them will find compassion.
PROVERBS 28:13 NASB

For one who knows the right thing to do and does not do it, for him it is sin.
JAMES 4:17 NASB

Confess your trespasses to one another, and pray for one another, that you may be healed. The effective, fervent prayer of a righteous man avails much.
JAMES 5:16 NKJV

If we confess our sins, he is faithful and just and will forgive us our sins and purify us from all unrighteousness.
1 JOHN 1:9 NIV

Whoever confesses that Jesus is the Son of God, God abides in him, and he in God.
1 JOHN 4:15 ESV

I acknowledged my sin to you,
and I did not cover my iniquity;
I said, "I will confess my transgressions to the LORD,"
and you forgave the iniquity of my sin.
PSALM 32:5 ESV

If you declare with your mouth, "Jesus is Lord," and believe in your heart that God raised him from the dead, you will be saved.
ROMANS 10:9 NIV

CONFIDENCE

"Have I not commanded you? Be strong and courageous. Do not be frightened, and do not be dismayed, for the LORD your God is with you wherever you go."
JOSHUA 1:9 ESV

The LORD will accomplish what concerns me;
Your faithfulness, LORD, is everlasting;
Do not abandon the works of Your hands.
PSALM 138:8 NASB

I am convinced that neither death, nor life, nor angels, nor principalities, nor things present, nor things to come, nor powers, nor height, nor depth, nor any other created thing will be able to separate us from the love of God that is in Christ Jesus our Lord.
ROMANS 8:38-39 NASB

Do not throw away your confidence, which has a great reward. For you have need of endurance, so that when you have done the will of God, you may receive what was promised.
HEBREWS 10:35-36 NASB

Let us then with confidence draw near to the throne of grace, that we may receive mercy and find grace to help in time of need.
HEBREWS 4:16 ESV

I can do all this through him who gives me strength.
PHILIPPIANS 4:13 NIV

The LORD will be at your side
and will keep your foot from being snared.
PROVERBS 3:26 NIV

CONFUSION

All of them are put to shame and confounded;
the makers of idols go in confusion together.
ISAIAH 45:16 ESV

"The Helper, the Holy Spirit whom the Father will send in My name, He will teach you all things, and remind you of all that I said to you."
JOHN 14:26 NASB

"When He, the Spirit of truth, has come, He will guide you into all truth; for He will not speak on His own authority, but whatever He hears He will speak; and He will tell you things to come."
JOHN 16:13 NKJV

God is not a God of confusion but of peace.
1 CORINTHIANS 14:33 ESV

Reflect on what I am saying, for the Lord will give you insight into all this.
2 TIMOTHY 2:7 NIV

Beloved, do not believe every spirit, but test the spirits to see whether they are from God, because many false prophets have gone out into the world.
1 JOHN 4:1 NASB

CONTENTMENT

"Beware, and be on your guard against every form of greed; for not even when one is affluent does his life consist of his possessions."
LUKE 12:15 NASB

Not that I speak in regard to need, for I have learned in whatever state I am, to be content: I know how to be abased, and I know how to abound. Everywhere and in all things I have learned both to be full and to be hungry, both to abound and to suffer need.
PHILIPPIANS 4:11-12 NKJV

Each person should live as a believer in whatever situation the Lord has assigned to them, just as God has called them.
1 CORINTHIANS 7:17 NIV

For the sake of Christ, then, I am content with weaknesses, insults, hardships, persecutions, and calamities. For when I am weak, then I am strong.
2 CORINTHIANS 12:10 ESV

Godliness actually is a means of great gain when accompanied by contentment. For we have brought nothing into the world, so we cannot take anything out of it, either. If we have food and covering, with these we shall be content. But those who want to get rich fall into temptation and a trap, and many foolish and harmful desires which plunge people into ruin and destruction.
1 TIMOTHY 6:6-9 NASB

DEBT

The LORD your God will have blessed you just as He has promised you, and you will lend to many nations, but you will not borrow; and you will rule over many nations, but they will not rule over you.
DEUTERONOMY 15:6 NASB

The wicked borrows and does not repay, But the righteous shows mercy and gives.
PSALM 37:21 NKJV

Pay to all what is owed to them: taxes to whom taxes are owed, revenue to whom revenue is owed, respect to whom respect is owed, honor to whom honor is owed.
ROMANS 13:7-8 ESV

Wealth gained hastily will dwindle, but whoever gathers little by little will increase it.
PROVERBS 13:11 ESV

It is better that you not vow, than vow and not pay.
ECCLESIASTES 5:5 NASB

"If you lend to those from whom you hope to receive back, what credit is that to you? For even sinners lend to sinners to receive as much back. But love your enemies, do good, and lend, hoping for nothing in return; and your reward will be great, and you will be sons of the Most High. For He is kind to the unthankful and evil."
LUKE 6:34-35 NKJV

"Suppose one of you wants to build a tower. Won't you first sit down and estimate the cost to see if you have enough money to complete it?"
LUKE 14:28 NIV

My God will supply all your needs according to His riches in glory in Christ Jesus.
PHILIPPIANS 4:19 NASB

DEPRESSION

The righteous cry out, and the LORD hears And rescues them from all their troubles. The LORD is near to the brokenhearted And saves those who are crushed in spirit.
PSALM 34:17-18 NASB

I waited patiently for the LORD;
And He inclined to me,
And heard my cry.
He also brought me up out of a horrible pit,
Out of the miry clay,
And set my feet upon a rock,
And established my steps.
PSALM 40:1-2 NKJV

Why, my soul, are you downcast?
Why so disturbed within me?
Put your hope in God,
for I will yet praise him,
my Savior and my God.
PSALM 42:5 NIV

When the cares of my heart are many,
your consolations cheer my soul.
PSALM 94:19 ESV

Answer me quickly, LORD, my spirit fails;
Do not hide Your face from me,
Or I will be the same as those who go
down to the pit.
Let me hear Your faithfulness in the
morning,
For I trust in You;
Teach me the way in which I should walk;
For to You I lift up my soul.
PSALM 143:7-8 NASB

May the God of hope fill you with all joy
and peace in believing, so that by the
power of the Holy Spirit you may abound
in hope.
ROMANS 15:13 ESV

Whatever is true, whatever is
honorable, whatever is right, whatever
is pure, whatever is lovely, whatever is
commendable, if there is any excellence
and if anything worthy of praise, think
about these things.
PHILIPPIANS 4:8 NASB

DELIVERANCE

I sought the LORD, and He heard me,
And delivered me from all my fears.
PSALM 34:4 NKJV

The righteous cry out, and the LORD
hears them;
he delivers them from all their troubles.
PSALM 34:17 NIV

"Call upon me in the day of trouble;
I will deliver you, and you shall glorify me."
PSALM 50:15 ESV

"You will know the truth, and the truth
will set you free."
JOHN 8:32 NASB

The Lord is faithful, who will establish you
and guard you from the evil one.
2 THESSALONIANS 3:3 NKJV

No temptation has overtaken you except
something common to mankind; and God
is faithful, so He will not allow you to be
tempted beyond what you are able, but
with the temptation will provide the way
of escape also, so that you will be able to
endure it.
1 CORINTHIANS 10:13 NASB

Then they cried out to the LORD in their
trouble,
And He delivered them out of their
distresses.
PSALM 107:6 NKJV

Submit yourselves, then, to God. Resist
the devil, and he will flee from you.
JAMES 4:7 NIV

The Lord will rescue me from every
evil deed and bring me safely into his
heavenly kingdom. To him be the glory
forever and ever. Amen.
2 TIMOTHY 4:18 ESV

DISCOURAGEMENT

"The LORD is the one who is going ahead of you; He will be with you. He will not desert you or abandon you. Do not fear and do not be dismayed."
DEUTERONOMY 31:8 NASB

Since we are surrounded by such a great cloud of witnesses, let us throw off everything that hinders and the sin that so easily entangles. And let us run with perseverance the race marked out for us.
HEBREWS 12:1 NIV

"Have I not commanded you? Be strong and of good courage; do not be afraid, nor be dismayed, for the LORD your God is with you wherever you go."
JOSHUA 1:9 NKJV

"I have told you these things, so that in me you may have peace. In this world you will have trouble. But take heart! I have overcome the world."
JOHN 16:33 NIV

My beloved brothers, be steadfast, immovable, always abounding in the work of the Lord, knowing that in the Lord your labor is not in vain.
1 CORINTHIANS 15:58 ESV

Our light affliction, which is but for a moment, is working for us a far more exceeding and eternal weight of glory, while we do not look at the things which are seen, but at the things which are not seen. For the things which are seen are temporary, but the things which are not seen are eternal.
2 CORINTHIANS 4:17-18 NKJV

FAITH

"Whatever you ask in prayer, you will receive, if you have faith."
MATTHEW 21:22 ESV

"With God nothing will be impossible."
LUKE 1:37 NKJV

Faith comes from hearing the message, and the message is heard through the word about Christ.
ROMANS 10:17 NIV

Jesus answered and said to them, "Have faith in God. Truly I say to you, whoever says to this mountain, 'Be taken up and thrown into the sea,' and does not doubt in his heart, but believes that what he says is going to happen, it will be granted to him. Therefore, I say to you, all things for which you pray and ask, believe that you have received them, and they will be granted to you."
MARK 11:22-24 NASB

We walk by faith, not by sight.
2 CORINTHIANS 5:7 ESV

Faith is the assurance of things hoped for, the conviction of things not seen.
HEBREWS 11:1 ESV

Without faith it is impossible to please Him, for the one who comes to God must believe that He exists, and that He proves to be One who rewards those who seek Him.
HEBREWS 11:6 NASB

You believe that God is one; you do well. Even the demons believe—and shudder!
JAMES 2:19 ESV

FEAR

The LORD is my light and my salvation;
Whom shall I fear?
The LORD is the strength of my life;
Of whom shall I be afraid?
PSALM 27:1 NKJV

The LORD is for me; I will not fear;
What can man do to me?
PSALM 118:6 NASB

"Do not fear, for I have redeemed you;
I have summoned you by name; you are
mine."
ISAIAH 43:1 NIV

When I am afraid, I put my trust in you.
PSALM 56:3 NIV

"Do not fear those who kill the body but
cannot kill the soul. But rather fear Him
who is able to destroy both soul and body
in hell."
MATTHEW 10:28 NKJV

For this reason I remind you to kindle
afresh the gift of God which is in you
through the laying on of my hands. For
God has not given us a spirit of timidity,
but of power and love and discipline.
2 TIMOTHY 1:6-7 NASB

There is no fear in love; but perfect love
casts out fear, because fear involves
torment. But he who fears has not been
made perfect in love.
1 JOHN 4:18 NKJV

FORGIVENESS

"I say to you who hear, Love your enemies,
do good to those who hate you."
LUKE 6:27 ESV

"Lord, how many times shall I forgive my
brother or sister who sins against me? Up
to seven times?"
Jesus answered, "I tell you, not seven
times, but seventy-seven times."
MATTHEW 18:21-22 NIV

"When you stand praying, if you hold
anything against anyone, forgive them, so
that your Father in heaven may forgive
you your sins."
MARK 11:25 NIV

"I, I am he who blots out your
transgressions for my own sake,
and I will not remember your sins."
ISAIAH 43:25 ESV

"If you do not forgive men their
trespasses, neither will your Father
forgive your trespasses."
MATTHEW 6:15 NKJV

All bitterness, wrath, anger, clamor, and
slander must be removed from you, along
with all malice. Be kind to one another,
compassionate, forgiving each other, just
as God in Christ also has forgiven you.
EPHESIANS 4:31-32 NASB

Bear with each other and forgive one
another if any of you has a grievance
against someone. Forgive as the Lord
forgave you.
COLOSSIANS 3:13 NIV

If we confess our sins, He is faithful and
just to forgive us our sins and to cleanse
us from all unrighteousness. If we say
that we have not sinned, we make Him a
liar, and His word is not in us.
1 JOHN 1:9-10 NKJV

GIVING

Honor the LORD with your wealth
and with the firstfruits of all your
produce;
then your barns will be filled with plenty,
and your vats will be bursting with wine.
PROVERBS 3:9-10 ESV

He who has pity on the poor lends to the
LORD,
And He will pay back what he has given.
PROVERBS 19:17 NKJV

"Give to everyone who asks of you, and
whoever takes away what is yours, do not
demand it back."
LUKE 6:30 NASB

"Give, and it will be given to you: good
measure, pressed down, shaken together,
and running over will be put into your
bosom. For with the same measure that
you use, it will be measured back to you."
LUKE 6:38 NKJV

In everything I did, I showed you that by
this kind of hard work we must help the
weak, remembering the words the Lord
Jesus himself said: "It is more blessed to
give than to receive."
ACTS 20:35 NIV

Each one must give as he has decided
in his heart, not reluctantly or under
compulsion, for God loves a cheerful giver.
2 CORINTHIANS 9:7 ESV

Do not forget to do good and to share,
for with such sacrifices God is well
pleased.
HEBREWS 13:16 NKJV

GUIDANCE

Make me know Your ways, LORD;
Teach me Your paths.
PSALM 25:4 NASB

The humble He guides in justice,
And the humble He teaches His way.
All the paths of the LORD are mercy and
truth,
To such as keep His covenant and His
testimonies.
PSALM 25:9-10 NKJV

The LORD makes firm the steps
of the one who delights in him;
though he may stumble, he will not fall,
for the LORD upholds him with his hand.
PSALM 37:23-24 NIV

Teach me the way in which I should walk;
For to You I lift up my soul.
PSALM 143:8 NASB

For lack of guidance a nation falls,
but victory is won through many
advisers.
PROVERBS 11:14 NIV

The LORD will guide you continually,
And satisfy your soul in drought,
And strengthen your bones;
You shall be like a watered garden,
And like a spring of water, whose waters
do not fail.
ISAIAH 58:11 NKJV

When the Spirit of truth comes, he will
guide you into all the truth, for he will not
speak on his own authority, but whatever
he hears he will speak, and he will declare
to you the things that are to come.
JOHN 16:13 ESV

The heart of man plans his way,
but the LORD establishes his steps.
PROVERBS 16:9 ESV

HEALING

"If my people who are called by my name
humble themselves, and pray and seek
my face and turn from their wicked ways,
then I will hear from heaven and will
forgive their sin and heal their land."
2 CHRONICLES 7:14 ESV

The LORD will sustain him upon his
sickbed;
In his illness, You restore him to health.
PSALM 41:3 NASB

Bless the LORD, O my soul,
And forget not all His benefits:
Who forgives all your iniquities,
Who heals all your diseases,
Who redeems your life from destruction,
Who crowns you with lovingkindness and
tender mercies.
PSALM 103:2-4 NKJV

He was pierced for our offenses,
He was crushed for our wrongdoings;
The punishment for our well-being was
laid upon Him,
And by His wounds we are healed.
ISAIAH 53:5 NASB

Heal me, O LORD, and I shall be healed;
Save me, and I shall be saved,
For You are my praise.
JEREMIAH 17:14 NKJV

He heals the brokenhearted
and binds up their wounds.
PSALM 147:3 NIV

Is anyone among you sick? Let him call
for the elders of the church, and let them
pray over him, anointing him with oil in
the name of the Lord. And the prayer
of faith will save the one who is sick, and
the Lord will raise him up. And if he has
committed sins, he will be forgiven.
JAMES 5:14-15 ESV

INTERCESSION

The Spirit helps us in our weakness. We
do not know what we ought to pray for,
but the Spirit himself intercedes for us
through wordless groans. And he who
searches our hearts knows the mind of
the Spirit, because the Spirit intercedes
for God's people in accordance with the
will of God.
ROMANS 8:26-27 NIV

Who is to condemn? Christ Jesus is the
one who died—more than that, who was
raised—who is at the right hand of God,
who indeed is interceding for us.
ROMANS 8:34 ESV

He is also able to save to the uttermost
those who come to God through
Him, since He always lives to make
intercession for them.
HEBREWS 7:25 NKJV

I urge, then, first of all, that petitions,
prayers, intercession and thanksgiving
be made for all people—for kings and
all those in authority, that we may live
peaceful and quiet lives in all godliness
and holiness. This is good, and pleases
God our Savior, who wants all people to
be saved and to come to a knowledge of
the truth. For there is one God and one

mediator between God and mankind, the man Christ Jesus,
1 TIMOTHY 2:1-5 NIV

JUDGMENT

"Judge not, that you be not judged. For with the judgment you pronounce you will be judged, and with the measure you use it will be measured to you.
MATTHEW 7:1-2 ESV

"Judge not, and you shall not be judged. Condemn not, and you shall not be condemned. Forgive, and you will be forgiven."
LUKE 6:37 NKJV

You have no excuse, O man, every one of you who judges. For in passing judgment on another you condemn yourself, because you, the judge, practice the very same things.
ROMANS 2:1 ESV

Why do you judge your brother? Or why do you show contempt for your brother? For we shall all stand before the judgment seat of Christ. For it is written:
"As I live, says the LORD,
Every knee shall bow to Me,
And every tongue shall confess to God."
So then each of us shall give account of himself to God.
ROMANS 14:10-12 NKJV

Judgment is without mercy to one who has shown no mercy. Mercy triumphs over judgment.
JAMES 2:13 ESV

"By your words you will be justified, and by your words you will be condemned."
MATTHEW 12:37 NASB

JUSTICE

To do righteousness and justice
Is more acceptable to the LORD than sacrifice.
PROVERBS 21:3 NKJV

When justice is done,
it brings joy to the righteous
but terror to evildoers.
PROVERBS 21:15 NIV

Learn to do good;
Seek justice,
Rebuke the oppressor,
Obtain justice for the orphan,
Plead for the widow's case.
ISAIAH 1:17 NASB

For the LORD is a God of justice;
Blessed are all those who wait for Him.
ISAIAH 30:18 NKJV

He has shown you, O mortal, what is good.
And what does the LORD require of you?
To act justly and to love mercy
and to walk humbly with your God.
MICAH 6:8 NIV

He who does wrong will be repaid
for what he has done, and there is no partiality.
COLOSSIANS 3:25 NKJV

We know him who said, "It is mine to avenge; I will repay," and again, "The Lord will judge his people."
HEBREWS 10:30 NIV

LONELINESS

"The LORD is the one who is going ahead of you; He will be with you. He will not

desert you or abandon you. Do not fear and do not be dismayed."
DEUTERONOMY 31:8 NASB

When my father and my mother forsake me,
Then the LORD will take care of me.
PSALM 27:10 NKJV

Where can I go from your Spirit?
Where can I flee from your presence?
If I go up to the heavens, you are there;
if I make my bed in the depths, you are there.
If I rise on the wings of the dawn,
if I settle on the far side of the sea,
even there your hand will guide me,
your right hand will hold me fast.
PSALM 139:7-10 NIV

At my first defense no one stood with me, but all forsook me. May it not be charged against them.
But the Lord stood with me and strengthened me, so that the message might be preached fully through me, and that all the Gentiles might hear. Also I was delivered out of the mouth of the lion.
2 TIMOTHY 4:16-17 NKJV

LOVE

Let love and faithfulness never leave you; bind them around your neck,
write them on the tablet of your heart.
Then you will win favor and a good name in the sight of God and man.
PROVERBS 3:3-4 NIV

"For God so loved the world, that he gave his only Son, that whoever believes in him should not perish but have eternal life."
JOHN 3:16 ESV

"Whoever has my commands and keeps them is the one who loves me. The one who loves me will be loved by my Father, and I too will love them and show myself to them."
JOHN 14:21 NIV

A friend loves at all times,
And a brother is born for adversity.
PROVERBS 17:17 NKJV

"I am giving you a new commandment, that you love one another; just as I have loved you, that you also love one another. By this all people will know that you are My disciples: if you have love for one another."
JOHN 13:34-35 NASB

Love suffers long and is kind; love does not envy; love does not parade itself, is not puffed up; does not behave rudely, does not seek its own, is not provoked, thinks no evil; does not rejoice in iniquity, but rejoices in the truth; bears all things, believes all things, hopes all things, endures all things.
Love never fails. But whether there are prophecies, they will fail; whether there are tongues, they will cease; whether there is knowledge, it will vanish away.
1 CORINTHIANS 13:4-8 NKJV

Do everything in love.
1 CORINTHIANS 16:14 NIV

Above all these put on love, which binds everything together in perfect harmony.
COLOSSIANS 3:14 ESV

God demonstrates His own love toward us, in that while we were still sinners, Christ died for us.
ROMANS 5:8 NASB

Dear friends, let us love one another, for love comes from God. Everyone who loves has been born of God and knows God. Whoever does not love does not know God, because God is love.
1 JOHN 4:7-8 NIV

PATIENCE

Be still before the LORD and wait patiently for him.
PSALM 37:7 ESV

I waited patiently for the LORD;
And He reached down to me and heard my cry.
PSALM 40:1 NASB

If we hope for what we do not see, through perseverance we wait eagerly for it.
ROMANS 8:25 NASB

Be patient, brethren, until the coming of the Lord. See how the farmer waits for the precious fruit of the earth, waiting patiently for it until it receives the early and latter rain. You also be patient. Establish your hearts, for the coming of the Lord is at hand.
JAMES 5:7-8 NKJV

They who wait for the LORD shall renew their strength;
they shall mount up with wings like eagles;
they shall run and not be weary;
they shall walk and not faint.
ISAIAH 40:31 ESV

Let us not grow weary while doing good, for in due season we shall reap if we do not lose heart.
GALATIANS 6:9 NKJV

PEACE

You will keep him in perfect peace,
Whose mind is stayed on You,
Because he trusts in You.
ISAIAH 26:3 NKJV

"I have told you these things, so that in me you may have peace. In this world you will have trouble. But take heart! I have overcome the world."
JOHN 16:33 NIV

Great peace have those who love your law; nothing can make them stumble.
PSALM 119:165 ESV

To set the mind on the flesh is death, but to set the mind on the Spirit is life and peace.
ROMANS 8:6 ESV

Strive for peace with everyone, and for the holiness without which no one will see the Lord.
HEBREWS 12:14 ESV

The fruit of righteousness is sown in peace by those who make peace.
JAMES 3:18 NASB

Be anxious for nothing, but in everything by prayer and supplication, with thanksgiving, let your requests be made known to God; and the peace of God, which surpasses all understanding, will guard your hearts and minds through Christ Jesus.
PHILIPPIANS 4:6-7 NKJV

God is not a God of confusion but of peace.
1 Corinthians 14:33 esv

May the God of hope fill you with all joy and peace as you trust in him, so that you may overflow with hope by the power of the Holy Spirit.
Romans 15:13 niv

May the Lord of peace himself give you peace at all times and in every way. The Lord be with all of you.
2 Thessalonians 3:16 niv

POVERTY

"There will never cease to be poor in the land. Therefore I command you, 'You shall open wide your hand to your brother, to the needy and to the poor, in your land.'"
Deuteronomy 15:11 esv

I have been young, and now am old;
Yet I have not seen the righteous forsaken,
Nor his descendants begging bread.
Psalm 37:25 nkjv

He raises the poor from the dust,
He lifts the needy from the garbage heap
To seat them with nobles, And He gives them a seat of honor as an inheritance;
For the pillars of the earth are the Lord's,
And He set the world on them.
1 Samuel 2:8 nasb

Do not love sleep, or you will become poor;
Open your eyes, and you will be satisfied with food.
Proverbs 20:13 nasb

The plans of the diligent lead surely to plenty,
But those of everyone who is hasty, surely to poverty.
Proverbs 21:5 nkjv

PRAYER

The righteous cry out, and the Lord hears them;
he delivers them from all their troubles.
Psalm 34:17 niv

"Call to Me, and I will answer you, and show you great and mighty things, which you do not know."
Jeremiah 33:3 nkjv

"When you pray, do not be like the hypocrites, for they love to pray standing in the synagogues and on the street corners to be seen by others. Truly I tell you, they have received their reward in full. But when you pray, go into your room, close the door and pray to your Father, who is unseen. Then your Father, who sees what is done in secret, will reward you. And when you pray, do not keep on babbling like pagans, for they think they will be heard because of their many words. Do not be like them, for your Father knows what you need before you ask him."
Matthew 6:5-8 niv

Confess your sins to one another, and pray for one another so that you may be healed. A prayer of a righteous person, when it is brought about, can accomplish much.
James 5:16 nasb

"I say to you, whatever things you ask when you pray, believe that you receive them, and you will have them."
MARK 11:24 NKJV

Pray in the Spirit on all occasions with all kinds of prayers and requests. With this in mind, be alert and always keep on praying for all the Lord's people.
EPHESIANS 6:18 NIV

Devote yourselves to prayer, keeping alert in it with an attitude of thanksgiving.
COLOSSIANS 4:2 NASB

Pray without ceasing.
1 THESSALONIANS 5:17 NKJV

PRIDE

When pride comes, then comes disgrace, but with humility comes wisdom.
PROVERBS 11:2 NIV

Pride goes before destruction, and a haughty spirit before a fall.
PROVERBS 16:18 ESV

A man's pride will bring him low, But the humble in spirit will retain honor.
PROVERBS 29:23 NKJV

Humble yourselves before the Lord, and he will exalt you.
JAMES 4:10 ESV

By the grace given to me I say to everyone among you not to think of himself more highly than he ought to think, but to think with sober judgment, each according to the measure of faith that God has assigned.
ROMANS 12:3 ESV

"He who glories, let him glory in the Lord." For not he who commends himself is approved, but whom the Lord commends.
2 CORINTHIANS 10:17-18 NKJV

If anyone thinks they are something when they are not, they deceive themselves.
GALATIANS 6:3 NIV

Do nothing from selfishness or empty conceit, but with humility consider one another as more important than yourselves.
PHILIPPIANS 2:3 NASB

PROSPERITY

Keep this Book of the Law always on your lips; meditate on it day and night, so that you may be careful to do everything written in it. Then you will be prosperous and successful.
JOSHUA 1:8 NIV

Taste and see that the LORD is good; How blessed is the man who takes refuge in Him!
Fear the LORD, you His saints; For to those who fear Him there is no lack of anything.
PSALM 34:8-9 NASB

Blessed are those who fear the LORD, who find great delight in his commands.
Their children will be mighty in the land; the generation of the upright will be blessed.
Wealth and riches are in their houses, and their righteousness endures forever.
PSALM 112:1-3 NIV

You shall eat the fruit of the labor of your hands;
you shall be blessed, and it shall be well with you.
PSALM 128:2 ESV

The LORD God is a sun and shield;
The LORD will give grace and glory;
No good thing will He withhold
From those who walk uprightly.
PSALM 84:11 NKJV

My God will supply all your needs according to His riches in glory in Christ Jesus.
PHILIPPIANS 4:19 NASB

PROTECTION

"The LORD will fight for you, and you have only to be silent."
EXODUS 14:14 ESV

Every word of God is pure;
He is a shield to those who put their trust in Him.
PROVERBS 30:5 NKJV

The LORD is good,
a stronghold in the day of trouble;
he knows those who take refuge in him.
NAHUM 1:7 ESV

It is better to take refuge in the LORD than to trust in humans.
PSALM 118:8 NIV

The name of the LORD is a strong tower;
The righteous runs into it and is safe.
PROVERBS 18:10 NASB

You, LORD, are a shield around me,
My glory, and the One who lifts my head.
PSALM 3:3 NASB

Though I walk in the midst of trouble,
you preserve my life;
you stretch out your hand against the wrath of my enemies,
and your right hand delivers me.
PSALM 138:7 ESV

The Lord is faithful, who will establish you and guard you from the evil one.
2 THESSALONIANS 3:3 NKJV

RIGHTEOUSNESS

The eyes of the LORD are on the righteous,
and his ears are attentive to their cry.
PSALM 34:15 NIV

Sow righteousness for yourselves,
reap the fruit of unfailing love,
and break up your unplowed ground;
for it is time to seek the LORD,
until he comes
and showers his righteousness on you.
HOSEA 10:12 NIV

God made him who had no sin to be sin for us, so that in him we might become the righteousness of God.
2 CORINTHIANS 5:21 NIV

To do righteousness and justice
Is more acceptable to the LORD than sacrifice.
PROVERBS 21:3 NKJV

We know that whoever is born of God does not sin; but he who has been born of God keeps himself, and the wicked one does not touch him.
1 JOHN 5:18 NKJV

Blessed are they who observe justice, who do righteousness at all times!
PSALM 106:3 ESV

SALVATION

"Very truly I tell you, no one can see the kingdom of God unless they are born again."
JOHN 3:3 NIV

"Truly, truly, I say to you, whoever hears my word and believes him who sent me has eternal life. He does not come into judgment, but has passed from death to life."
JOHN 5:24 ESV

"For God so loved the world, that He gave His only Son, so that everyone who believes in Him will not perish, but have eternal life. For God did not send the Son into the world to judge the world, but so that the world might be saved through Him. The one who believes in Him is not judged; the one who does not believe has been judged already, because he has not believed in the name of the only Son of God."
JOHN 3:16-18 NASB

If you confess with your mouth the Lord Jesus and believe in your heart that God has raised Him from the dead, you will be saved. For with the heart one believes unto righteousness, and with the mouth confession is made unto salvation.
ROMANS 10:9-10 NKJV

It is by grace you have been saved, through faith—and this is not from yourselves, it is the gift of God—not by works, so that no one can boast.
EPHESIANS 2:8-9 NIV

"Salvation is found in no one else, for there is no other name under heaven given to mankind by which we must be saved."
ACTS 4:12 NIV

SIN

Create in me a pure heart, O God, and renew a steadfast spirit within me.
PSALM 51:10 NIV

"What comes out of a man, that defiles a man. For from within, out of the heart of men, proceed evil thoughts, adulteries, fornications, murders, thefts, covetousness, wickedness, deceit, lewdness, an evil eye, blasphemy, pride, foolishness. All these evil things come from within and defile a man."
MARK 7:20-23 NKJV

The wages of sin is death, but the free gift of God is eternal life in Christ Jesus our Lord.
ROMANS 6:23 ESV

If we deliberately keep on sinning after we have received the knowledge of the truth, no sacrifice for sins is left.
HEBREWS 10:26 NIV

For one who knows the right thing to do and does not do it, for him it is sin.
JAMES 4:17 NASB

If we say that we have no sin, we deceive ourselves, and the truth is not in us. If we confess our sins, He is faithful and just to forgive us our sins and to cleanse us from all unrighteousness. If we say that we have not sinned, we make Him a liar, and His word is not in us.
1 JOHN 1:8-10 NKJV

Whoever conceals his transgressions will not prosper,
but he who confesses and forsakes them will obtain mercy.
PROVERBS 28:13 ESV

SPEAKING

Set a guard, O LORD, over my mouth;
keep watch over the door of my lips!
PSALM 141:3 ESV

The heart of the righteous weighs its answers,
but the mouth of the wicked gushes evil.
PROVERBS 15:28 NIV

Like apples of gold in settings of silver,
Is a word spoken at the proper time.
PROVERBS 25:11 NASB

A fool vents all his feelings,
But a wise man holds them back.
PROVERBS 29:11 NKJV

"By your words you will be acquitted, and by your words you will be condemned."
MATTHEW 12:37 NIV

Let no corrupting talk come out of your mouths, but only such as is good for building up, as fits the occasion, that it may give grace to those who hear.
EPHESIANS 4:29 ESV

Let your speech always be with grace, seasoned with salt, that you may know how you ought to answer each one.
COLOSSIANS 4:6 NKJV

Know this, my beloved brothers: let every person be quick to hear, slow to speak, slow to anger.
JAMES 1:19 ESV

No one among mankind can tame the tongue; it is a restless evil, full of deadly poison. With it we bless our Lord and Father, and with it we curse people, who have been made in the likeness of God; from the same mouth come both blessing and cursing. My brothers and sisters, these things should not be this way.
JAMES 3:8-10 NASB

SPIRITUAL WARFARE

Be sober, be vigilant; because your adversary the devil walks about like a roaring lion, seeking whom he may devour. Resist him, steadfast in the faith, knowing that the same sufferings are experienced by your brotherhood in the world.
1 PETER 5:8-9 NKJV

Though we live in the world, we do not wage war as the world does. The weapons we fight with are not the weapons of the world. On the contrary, they have divine power to demolish strongholds. We demolish arguments and every pretension that sets itself up against the knowledge of God, and we take captive every thought to make it obedient to Christ.
2 CORINTHIANS 10:3-5 NIV

We do not wrestle against flesh and blood, but against the rulers, against the authorities, against the cosmic powers over this present darkness, against the spiritual forces of evil in the heavenly places.
EPHESIANS 6:12 ESV

Submit therefore to God. But resist the devil, and he will flee from you.
JAMES 4:7 NASB

STRENGTH

The LORD is my strength and my shield;
My heart trusts in Him, and I am helped;
Therefore my heart triumphs,
And with my song I shall thank Him.
The LORD is their strength,
And He is a refuge of salvation to His
anointed.
PSALM 28:7-8 NASB

Those who wait for the LORD
Will gain new strength;
They will mount up with wings like eagles,
They will run and not get tired,
They will walk and not become weary.
ISAIAH 40:31 NASB

"My grace is sufficient for you, for My
strength is made perfect in weakness."
2 CORINTHIANS 12:9 NKJV

My flesh and my heart may fail,
but God is the strength of my heart
and my portion forever.
PSALM 73:26 NIV

He gives power to the faint,
and to him who has no might
he increases strength.
ISAIAH 40:29 ESV

Be of good courage,
And He shall strengthen your heart,
All you who hope in the LORD.
PSALM 31:24 NKJV

SURRENDER

He went a little beyond them, and fell to
the ground and began praying that if it
were possible, the hour might pass Him
by. And He was saying, "Abba! Father!
All things are possible for You; remove
this cup from Me; yet not what I will, but
what You will."
MARK 14:35-36 NASB

I urge you, brothers and sisters, in view
of God's mercy, to offer your bodies
as a living sacrifice, holy and pleasing
to God—this is your true and proper
worship. Do not conform to the pattern
of this world, but be transformed by the
renewing of your mind. Then you will be
able to test and approve what God's will
is—his good, pleasing and perfect will.
ROMANS 12:1-2 NIV

Calling the crowd to him with his
disciples, he said to them, "If anyone
would come after me, let him deny
himself and take up his cross and follow
me. For whoever would save his life will
lose it, but whoever loses his life for my
sake and the gospel's will save it."
MARK 8:34-35 ESV

TEMPTATION

No temptation has overtaken you except
something common to mankind; and God
is faithful, so He will not allow you to be
tempted beyond what you are able, but
with the temptation will provide the way
of escape also, so that you will be able to
endure it.
1 CORINTHIANS 10:13 NASB

Walk in the Spirit, and you shall not fulfill
the lust of the flesh. For the flesh lusts
against the Spirit, and the Spirit against
the flesh; and these are contrary to one
another, so that you do not do the things
that you wish.
GALATIANS 5:16-17 NKJV

We do not have a High Priest who cannot sympathize with our weaknesses, but was in all points tempted as we are, yet without sin.
HEBREWS 4:15 NKJV

Blessed is the man who remains steadfast under trial, for when he has stood the test he will receive the crown of life, which God has promised to those who love him. Let no one say when he is tempted, "I am being tempted by God," for God cannot be tempted with evil, and he himself tempts no one. But each person is tempted when he is lured and enticed by his own desire. Then desire when it has conceived gives birth to sin, and sin when it is fully grown brings forth death.
JAMES 1:12-15 ESV

"Watch and pray so that you will not fall into temptation. The spirit is willing, but the flesh is weak."
MATTHEW 26:41 NIV

TRUST

Those who know your name trust in you, for you, LORD, have never forsaken those who seek you.
PSALM 9:10 NIV

Trust in him at all times, you people; pour out your hearts to him, for God is our refuge.
PSALM 62:8 NIV

Trust in the LORD with all your heart, and do not lean on your own understanding.
In all your ways acknowledge him, and he will make straight your paths.
PROVERBS 3:5-6 ESV

Trust in the LORD forever, For in God the LORD, we have an everlasting Rock.
ISAIAH 26:4 NASB

Commit your way to the LORD, Trust also in Him, and He will do it.
PSALM 37:5 NASB

Blessed is the one who trusts in the LORD, whose confidence is in him.
They will be like a tree planted by the water
that sends out its roots by the stream.
It does not fear when heat comes; its leaves are always green.
It has no worries in a year of drought and never fails to bear fruit."
JEREMIAH 17:7-8 NIV

TRUTH

Teach me your way, O LORD, that I may walk in your truth; unite my heart to fear your name.
PSALM 86:11 ESV

The LORD is near to all who call on Him, To all who call on Him in truth.
PSALM 145:18 NASB

"You shall know the truth, and the truth shall make you free."
JOHN 8:32 NKJV

"When he, the Spirit of truth, comes, he will guide you into all the truth."
JOHN 16:13 NIV

Ridding yourselves of falsehood, speak truth each one of you with his neighbor, because we are parts of one another.
EPHESIANS 4:25 NASB

VICTORY

"The LORD your God is the one who goes with you to fight for you against your enemies to give you victory."
DEUTERONOMY 20:4 NIV

In all these things we are more than conquerors through Him who loved us.
ROMANS 8:37 NKJV

Thanks be to God!
He gives us the victory through
our Lord Jesus Christ.
Therefore, my dear brothers and sisters,
stand firm. Let nothing move you.
Always give yourselves fully
to the work of the Lord,
because you know that your
labor in the Lord is not in vain.
1 CORINTHIANS 15:57-58 NIV

The weapons of our warfare are not of the flesh but have divine power to destroy strongholds.
2 CORINTHIANS 10:4 ESV

Whatever is born of God overcomes the world. And this is the victory that has overcome the world—our faith.
1 JOHN 5:4 NKJV

VISION

Plans fail for lack of counsel,
but with many advisers they succeed.
PROVERBS 15:22 NIV

The mind of a person plans his way,
But the LORD directs his steps.
PROVERBS 16:9 NASB

Where there is no revelation,
the people cast off restraint;

But happy is he who keeps the law.
PROVERBS 29:18 NKJV

For still the vision awaits its appointed time;
it hastens to the end—it will not lie.
If it seems slow, wait for it;
it will surely come; it will not delay."
HABAKKUK 2:3 ESV

WISDOM

The fear of the LORD is the beginning of wisdom;
A good understanding have all those who do His commandments.
His praise endures forever.
PSALM 111:10 NKJV

Blessed are those who find wisdom,
those who gain understanding,
for she is more profitable than silver
and yields better returns than gold.
PROVERBS 3:13-14 NIV

The way of a fool is right in his own eyes, but a wise man listens to advice.
PROVERBS 12:15 ESV

If any of you lacks wisdom, you should ask God, who gives generously to all without finding fault, and it will be given to you.
JAMES 1:5 NIV

Who is wise and understanding among you? By his good conduct let him show his works in the meekness of wisdom.
JAMES 3:13 ESV

The wisdom from above is first pure, then peace-loving, gentle, reasonable, full of mercy and good fruits, impartial, free of hypocrisy.
JAMES 3:17 NASB

WORTH

You created my innermost parts;
You wove me in my mother's womb.
I will give thanks to You, because I am
awesomely and wonderfully made;
Wonderful are Your works,
And my soul knows it very well.
PSALM 139:13-14 NASB

"Are not five sparrows sold for two
pennies? Yet not one of them is
forgotten by God. Indeed, the very hairs
of your head are all numbered. Don't be
afraid; you are worth more than many
sparrows."
LUKE 12:6-7 NIV

"You did not choose Me, but I chose you
and appointed you that you should go
and bear fruit, and that your fruit should
remain, that whatever you ask the Father
in My name He may give you."
JOHN 15:16 NKJV

You are a chosen people, a royal
priesthood, a holy nation, God's special
possession, that you may declare the
praises of him who called you out of
darkness into his wonderful light.
1 PETER 2:9 NIV